THE JOHN SCOTT
TILE COLLECTION

Front cover image: Encaustic tile depicting Medusa, Minton & Co., 1895, 15 diameter *(see p.354)*.

Compiled and edited by Gillian Crumpton.
Designed by Jemma Cox.
Cover designed by Katie Beard.

All photographs taken by David Houlston, D.J. Houlston Photography (with the exception of John Scott's Reception Room on pp.8–9, taken by Michael Whiteway, and the Salvador Dali Tiles on p.351, taken by Barbara Taylor).

ISBN 978-1-84165-623-6   1/17

Pitkin Publishing, The History Press, The Mill, Brimscombe Port, Stroud, Gloucestershire, GL5 2QG.
www.thehistorypress.co.uk

CONTENTS

FOREWORD

By Gillian Crumpton, Curator

I first became aware of John Scott and his involvement with the Museum in 2010 whilst sorting through some paperwork from the 1980s that I had found in an old filing cabinet belonging to a previous curator. In 1983 John, a property developer, had helped the Museum negotiate the purchase of the original Craven Dunnill & Co. tile factory. This building went on to become Jackfield Tile Museum.

Since then it seems that in every letter that he wrote to the Museum, John declared his ambition for Jackfield to be 'the greatest tile museum in the world'. Having this support in the early days must have been incredibly important and encouraging to the staff working to establish the collection and create a new museum.

I became the Curator of Jackfield Tile Museum in 2010 and found that this advocate for the Museum was still proclaiming the same ambition. A man of action and not just words, in 2012 John Scott decided to donate his entire collection of tiles to the Ironbridge Gorge Museum Trust for display at Jackfield. This is one of the finest private collections of mid-19th to mid-20th-century English decorative tiles in the country. It comprises around 1,700 pieces and represents the work of some of the best-known designers and manufacturers from that period.

In August 2013 a team from the Museum went to London to oversee the packing of the collection. I was completely overwhelmed as I stepped through the Gothic front door into John Scott's home. I can only describe it as a treasure trove of decorative arts, incorporating furniture, metalwork, sculpture, glassware, ceramics, and – of course – tiles. We engaged a fine art moving company who packed the collection over three days whilst we documented and watched every piece being carefully boxed up ready for transportation to Shropshire. John and his wife Takko were wonderfully accommodating and calm as we worked our way through their domestic sanctuary extracting all the tiles and tile panels. We left their house and London thoroughly exhausted but thrilled to know that a world-class collection of tiles was heading to the Museum. A few days later we watched as all 66 boxes and 306 tile panels were unloaded into our stores at Jackfield Tile Museum. The real work was yet to begin.

Before we even thought about display we had to catalogue the entire collection. We discussed the project with The National Association of Decorative & Fine Arts Societies from Wrekin, Shrewsbury and Wolverhampton and they were interested in working with us. We started work in November 2013. Each tile had to be cleaned, measured, condition-checked, described and given a unique number for our database. We met every Wednesday morning and Thursday afternoon, with six volunteers in each session. We finished the project after 450 hours of work from the volunteers. I am so thankful to have had such a wonderful, dedicated and passionate group of volunteers to work with Tamsin Bapty, Curator, and I on this project.

The next stage of the process was to have the tiles photographed to publication standard by David Houlston. David has worked with the Museum for many years and it made our job so much easier to work with an experienced professional who understands how museums work and who is sensitive to the collections.

The space that was to be transformed into a new permanent gallery for the collection had once been the Faience Department for Craven Dunnill & Co. This space had not been redeveloped with the rest of the Museum and had become a disused storage area, which meant we had a blank canvas to work with. In the gallery we hoped to generate a feeling for John's house and give a real impression of the collection from a collector's point of view, an angle that hadn't been explored previously in the Museum. We chose to recreate some of the ways in which John had displayed his collection and highlight his favourite tiles (a challenge with a collector, as favourites can change!) and the prominent designers represented in the collection. The end result is a space that is peaceful and that has a special atmosphere – one that I hope highlights the beautiful jewel-like tiles.

Since 1960 John has kept a meticulous record of what he has collected, what was paid for each item and where it came from, along with any interesting stories that might relate to the item. His personal catalogue is now several large volumes in extent. Many tiles were bought in mint condition, while some had to have the cement prised off their backs with hammer and chisel. Some were bought from well-known London dealers, while others were acquired from the characters he met at the markets of Portobello Road. John was able to salvage some from buildings that were due to be demolished as London was rebuilt in the 1960s and 70s; others still were gifts from friends and collectors.

The designs range from religious texts and iconography to fantastic sailing ships and mythical beasts; from dynamic examples of 1930s 'machine age' imagery to high modernism. In addition to this, almost the entire range of manufacturing methods are represented, which makes the collection hugely important for those interested in both style and technique.

In creating this catalogue we felt that it was important not only to show the entire breadth of the collection, but to organise it akin to the layout of John's house. This should give an idea of how he chose to display the tiles within this private sphere. As such, each chapter represents a different room or area within his home. The personal stories about his hunt for specific tiles, his anecdotes about dealers, and his thoughts about what draws him to certain designs, all add an extra dimension to these beautiful objects, and allow a certain amount of insight into the rationale behind his collection.

John's tiles are colourful, dramatic, beautiful and, most importantly, inspiring. The pieces are of the highest quality and represent many of the key names in English design and tile manufacture. The collection also reflects John as an individual and tells the story of 'the collector'. It has been an absolute pleasure to work on such a wonderful exhibition and I hope that through this catalogue and the gallery itself, readers and visitors will enjoy what is one of the most impressive personal collections of tiles in the country.

THE JOHN SCOTT COLLECTION AT JACKFIELD TILE MUSEUM

Founded in 1967, the Ironbridge Gorge Museum Trust Ltd is a registered charity whose twin aims are education and heritage conservation. The Trust cares for 36 scheduled monuments and listed buildings within the Ironbridge Gorge World Heritage Site and operates 10 museums which collectively tell the story of the birthplace of the Industrial Revolution.

The Trust is in the privileged and unusual position of having its entire collections Designated of national importance. The collection at Jackfield Tile Museum explores the tile industries of the Ironbridge Gorge from the 18th century to the present day. Jackfield was once at the centre of decorative tile production. The renowned manufacturers Craven Dunnill & Co. and Maw & Co. were based in this area, and the tiles and ceramics produced in their factories travelled around the world to adorn the walls and floors of Indian palaces, South African banks, and even the London Underground. The collection is focussed on the products and history of Craven Dunnill & Co. and Maw & Co. but also includes some examples from most of the other major Victorian factories in this country. The significance of the collection is greatly increased by housing and displaying it in the most complete surviving Victorian decorative tile factory in the UK.

The Trust strives to collect pieces by significant artists and manufacturers, and show the evolution of decorative techniques, manufacturing processes, and the changing fashions in tile and ceramic design. John Scott's generous donation of his tile collection will help the Museum meet its ambition of becoming a world centre for 19th- and 20th-century English decorative tiles.

This catalogue would not have been possible without the support of John Scott. The Trust would also like to thank: Chris Blanchett, who has so generously provided advice and comment on the tiles and text; the Tiles & Architectural Ceramics Society; The National Association of Decorative & Fine Arts Societies; and finally, The Worshipful Company of Tylers and Bricklayers.

With the exception of the Salvador Dali tiles, all photography is by David Houlston, of D.J. Houlston Photography, who has worked with the Museum for many years.

NOTE ON FORMAT

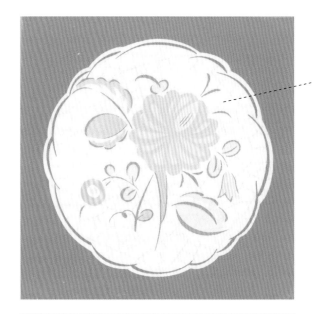

Description; where known the
designer and manufacturer have
been included; where known
the date of production has been
included; all sizes are in inches;
for framed works the overall
framed size is given

Image of tile

Hand-painted tile, designed by Truda Carter for
Carter & Co., 1950s, 6 x 6

JS2013.527.315

The black field was very appealing and I adore the light
touch of the painter. Carter tiles are almost always
attractive as they choose excellent artists.

Unique identifying number

Where given a comment from John Scott has been
included; these comments are at times duplicated
across different tiles

N.B. Variations can occur within the names of tile companies

MY TILE COLLECTION
By John Scott

I start by a declaration of shame. Maybe I can excuse myself by stating that I never anticipated having to produce a catalogue. So, all the facts – prices paid, details of makers, designers – precisely those matters that the tile enthusiasts want are often missing. Why? Because my catalogue was made for fun and not for public examination! I decided to write up everything I bought with details of date, price, vendor etc. And I stuck a sticker on every purchase. My first entry is dated 22 October 1961.

Two problems have arisen on the tiles. One, the stickers have fallen off (no longer are things made to last like the notes stuck on the wonderful finds from Tutankhamun's tomb!) and many of my tiles are framed and high up on the wall. So I humbly apologise to my readers.

I have given talks on my collection. These give me great pleasure, enabling a natural conceit to have free expression. Many times I have been asked, 'Why do you collect?' After much cogitation I confess that it is loneliness. The things I collect are like old friends, always smiling and ever capricious. Some of them I love more than others, but that's life. Many of them evoke in my mind happy memories and joyful times with good friends. We were taught at school to have a hobby and I think everyone should have a hobby. It's just that mine is rather large! 'And what was your first item?' A small Chinese ivory skull. It was given to me by Max Reny-Smith, a Birkenhead solicitor. His collection was housed in a suite of rooms in a Rock Ferry hotel. He liked to show me a gold cigarette case with an exquisite enamel nude – signed by King Farouk of Egypt. I shall never forget the occasion. I was ten at the time.

Away at school aged 16 I remember saving a small Roland Hilder print from the dustbin to fill a blank wall. National Service saw me in Malaya with the 10th Gurkhas and I can think of no collecting enthusiasm then save an unfulfilled desire to own a Malay kris. Patrolling in the jungle and rugby were my main activities; there was a combined All Malaya rugby tour to Bangkok. I remember only two aspects: the colossal Fijians who enabled us to win all our matches. The Fijian regiment was never beaten during their entire tour of duty in Malaya. I played in the only team that managed a draw. (But I digress. It is very easy and often that I am diverted onto fascinating stories that take me off the main track. I think this is the nature of the game of collecting.) The second memory, from the rugby tour to Thailand, is the discovery of a 14th-century bronze Buddha's head. It is only one-inch high and I had a modest wood stand made for it. There it is now, sitting on my mantelpiece, exuding nostalgia.

Next came three years of paradise at Oxford. My only claim to fame is that I was admitted without exam or interview. As my first attempt at O levels had produced only three passes, I knew obtaining a degree would be a severe trial. It was. I only got a Third! So it was all rugby and studies. But I did read Gibbon's *The Decline and Fall of the Roman Empire*. This edition was fully illustrated with Piranese engravings. Thus I made my first serious 'art' purchase – the frontispiece of Vedute di Roma by Jean Baptiste Piranese … £3.50. Now I have 50 of them … love them all … never tired of any.

1959: left Oxford – articled clerk in a solicitor's office – lived in a bedsitter, 3 Addison Gardens W14 – shared bathroom and fridge and cooker on third floor landing … great … few cares in the world … and freedom. I started visiting Portobello Road Market before Saturday's rugby.

The most significant date in my collecting was 1961 when my dear Uncle Eric loaned me £2,650 to buy 84 Hammersmith Bridge Road. I had to furnish it. The first entry in the first Collection Book reads 'Oct '60 1 pair of early Victorian dining chairs Regency House Portobello Road £4 10s' (that's £4.50 in today's money). So, the main focus of my 'collecting' was furniture and glass. Glass, because a bottle of Bull's Blood (Rioja – 4/6d = 25p) from Old Compton Street, Soho spoke a lot tastier from a nice 18th-century tall Wrythen ale glass. So, I now feel I should divulge to my readers that tiles are not the totality of my collection.

I think of glass being my first collection and I certainly like to use my drinking glasses frequently. Then, furniture, which was a necessity in the little house in Hammersmith. I have had a long-standing love of metal-work, particularly cast-iron as it was such a powerful element in Victorian times when we were great. Sculpture was set in my subliminal brain on account of the proximity of the Lady Lever Art Gallery to my home town of Birkenhead. Then ceramics. This includes tiles but is a generic term covering an enormous area. My ceramic collection is very narrow and I seek those pieces designed by architects – A.W.N. Pugin, Dr Christopher Dresser, C.F.A. Voysey, G.E. Street, Bruce Talbot, Owen Jones, John P. Seddon and many others.

It is the quality of the design and manufacturer that has drawn me towards these top architect/designers. And the more I look at these tiles the more I feel justification in this major belief and assertion: the greatest tile makers in the world flourished in this country between 1830 and 1930. Whatever the reader may feel I hope this bold assertion will be the start of much discussion. I have never believed comparisons are odious; here I hope they will be forceful and instructive, interesting and provocative.

The first tile entry in the Collection Book was 10 August 1968: '6" square tile by William De Morgan 2 variegated blue carnation flowers in duo tone green foliage Merton Abbey bought from Richard Dennis £4 – asking £5!' (See JS2013.527.559, p.337.) This was after I had sold my Hammersmith House for £6,850 in 1966 (I thought I was very clever having created a nice patio and laid the cork floor but it was pure inflation!) and had bought 79 Portobello Road for £11,000. This again was significant in two respects: one, I started my property career by creating a ground-floor shop and letting it; two, I had a nice maisonette in the heart of that fabulous market. Unmarried and without a 'partner', I had time to work, play rugby and … collect!

My love of tiles was all because of John Cox. We both played for The Harlequins, long before the advent of the professional game. A bit of what they call 'bonding' today took place when playing for the Harlequins 2nd VII – we beat the 1st VII in the final of the Esher 7-a-side rugby competition. I shall resist the temptation to describe in detail how we got past the famous England full back Bob Hiller. John collected 17th- and 18th-century Dutch tiles and I followed him around. He taught me a lot and naturally I bought a few and liked them. I would say the Dutch were the greatest tile makers and decorators for 100 or so years before our ascendancy. I often thought how much the Dutch housewife must have pestered her man to tile the kitchen; then the larder and on and on … A rich citizen can afford to indulge the demanding lady of the house – and the Dutch were very rich with their huge navy, extensive worldwide colonies and hard work.

Tile Number 168 (JS2013.527.7 on p.15) is a charming Liverpool transfer print of a sailing ship at anchor in a Caribbean cove, and reminds me of my jaunts with John Cox.

From the middle to the late 60s I concentrated on English tiles. The reason is simply that I love England. I joke with those who will tolerate me that I am the last of the Empire loyalists! English people should collect English things. People should collect things of their own country – something to be proud of. Having said that, of course, a lot of people collect English things. We just produced such a huge volume of stuff! On reflection, I recollect that my first tile purchase was not for £4 from Richard Dennis. It was two shillings from a Portobello junk stall – at the north end before the flyover was built. It was too insignificant to be catalogued. My tile purchase from Richard Dennis was only because of my glass collection (Richard was originally a specialist glass seller). I was buying Gallé vases and chanced upon De Morgan. I remember later, in the 70s and 80s, trying to persuade Michael Whiteway to stock tiles. 'I don't like tile people; they spend too much time talking and arguing about the price.' Now Michael is selling encaustics for £10 each!

I started this by confessing to my useless cataloguing style. Now I must confess that my collection does not cover the vast range of tile manufacturers. It is impossible to record them all. My collection is merely a few snapshots in a long film. At least there is a huge area of choice for new tile collectors. You should get yourself a good computer. To be able to call up eight full-colour encaustic tiles or an A.W.N. Pugin design will be a great bonus. But although there are vast areas in the field of English tiles as yet uncovered – indeed undiscovered – there is no need to collect tiles. You will need an inquisitive eye and mind to seek out what you would enjoy collecting. All I can wish for you is 'good hunting' and when you've found what you want to collect, keep going. The more you do, the more you will love it. But have a hobby and may it be ... collecting!

So ... you've decided to collect tiles. The best ones are always covered in plaster or cement. You will want to remove it. I shall never forget a lesson in this field from Eddie Phillips in his shop at 99 Portobello Road. I was explaining how the price of ten encaustics with half an inch of cement on the back could not be more than £5 each (he was asking £10). He laid one on the floor (you can see the tiled pavement he laid in the shop now) and struck its back with a chisel. The cement flew off like water off a duck's back. So, it can be done. I use a very wide flat chisel and a caborundum tip on a hand drill. My method takes ages but I enjoy the work – a little exercise and very satisfying. Minton encaustics are very tough and cheap-ish. De Morgans are easily broken and very expensive. As my readers will note, encaustic tiles are close to my heart. Unglazed examples I polish with clear wax and a little water – it was always called 'spit and polish' and it really works. The glistening finish is very beautiful and enlivens the designs in the tile. I hope the tiles on display will set a good example. Many tiles that 'make a pattern' may require (depending on how you wish to display your collection) a frame, and border tiles to set them off. Jon Catleugh, who had the finest collection of De Morgan tiles ever, set his tiles on boards covered in oatmeal cloth. It was excellent. Your own display will enable you to introduce your own taste. The Victorians set tiles into furniture extensively.

I was lucky enough to see Sir Frank Bowden's collection of Japanese armour, then considered the best in the world. He had a sword made by one of the top masters of that speciality of those wonderful people. Crudely cut into the blade was an image of three criminals tied together. They had felt it an honour to test the blade. He also owned a centipede embalmed in a six-inch column of gum from a tree that was 5 million years old.

I met Arthur Chesser during my rummagings in Portobello Market. He used to work for Pollards who made and fitted those fabulous bronze decorative shop fronts in Regent, Oxford and Bond streets. He had some wonderful coins: an enormous silver one with Charles I on horseback, then a Spanish doubloon cut in two and over-stamped with a value of a sovereign. Arthur always said, 'if the only thing wrong with an object is the price, BUY IT'. I would only add you should have the money to pay and not rely on borrowing!

I shall permit myself a personal digression from years back. I have always liked Lawrence Alma-Tadema. Suddenly in 1973 I had made quite a lot of money (on paper!!) in a joint property company. The other shareholder agreed to let me buy 'The Coign of Vantage' by Alma-Tadema. It was £20,000 and they lent me the money. Very shortly afterwards the property market collapsed and I had to sell. Result – loss of £7,000! It is now a major attraction in the Getty Museum in Malibu ... value £2 million. That was a good and painful lesson. Having said that, the greatest regret in the world of collecting is for those things you left behind because they were 'a bit too much'. Fortune favours the brave. If you buy quality you will never, in time, say 'I paid too much for that one'.

Collecting is like fishing. The one that got away is always the largest. So it is with me. And like Lot's wife one should never look back. But I cannot occasionally stop shedding a tear over the Zuloaga vases. Those were commissioned by Alfred Morrison (Alfred's father James Morrison was probably the richest commoner in 19th-century Britain and Alfred was his second son). The vases were made by Plácido Zuloaga and delivered to Morrison in 1877. Their design was heavily influenced by two pieces from the Alhambra Palace in Granada. The artistic bravura and technical virtuosity manifested in Zuloaga's work is truly breathtaking. The profusion of gold and silver inlay is a tour de force of damascene art and a magnificent homage to the Islamic models on which they were based. Morrison commissioned these vases to display with his oriental ceramics in his fabulous house Fonthill. They were designed by Owen Jones and made of forged iron inlaid with gold and silver. I could have bought these for £13,000 in 1974 but I was near bankruptcy after the property collapse. Today they are worth at least £2 million. Consequently, my funds were dramatically reduced but the urge to collect still ran strong. Hence the modest encaustic tile – an object of great beauty, excellent design, superbly made … and cheap!

Always try to buy the best. The more experience you acquire, the more you will recognise a rarity. It may be a bit too expensive but if you 'average' the price out over all your collection it will seem cheap. Can you guess my greatest 'find'? It certainly was unique!

As I struggle with my collection, trying to pull it together in type, age and image, and go through my voluminous library, I am drowned by the task. There is certainly an amazing range of books on the subject. I started with *The Decorated Tile: An Illustrated History of English Tile-making and Design* by J. and B. Austwick and the 1991 Fired Earth Exhibition. Among the dealers I like best are Richard Dennis, Michael Whiteway and Adrian Grater, and, if you are keen, join the excellent Tiles & Architectural Ceramics Society (TACS). Their annual Tile Fair is the highlight of my life. Approximately 50 members meet and display their tiles. We buy and sell; the camaraderie is delightful. We all love tiles. We travel to Nottingham and swap information, news and tiles. Michael Blood entertains us with glorious grub and a view of his spectacular tile collection. You should join TACS!

One vast area of mystery remains – who designed all these wonderful creations? We are indebted to the 'Patterns of Minton, Hollins, & Co.'s Encaustic Tiles, G. Edmund Street, Esq., R.A. 1881' containing over 150 tile designs. But did Street design all these? An enormous area of investigation awaits the aspirant tile lover. So … good hunting to you.

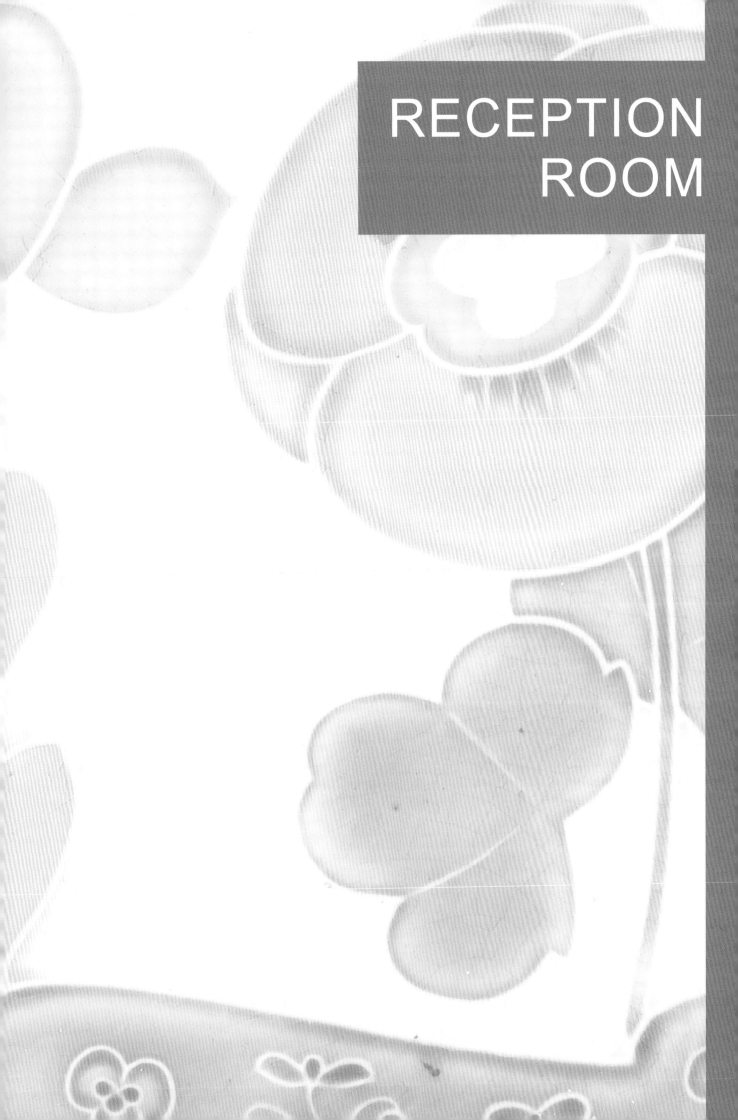

RECEPTION ROOM

Blue and white encaustic tile, Maw & Co., c.1880, 4¼ x 4¼

JS2013.527.9

Bought for almost pure vanity as an 'S' for Scott; but also a well-designed figure, not up to Eric Gill's class but well-designed nonetheless.

Sgraffito tile, Quentin Bell, Fulham Pottery, c.1970, 4 x 4

JS2013.527.10

Designed by Quentin Bell at a party given by Andy Tilbrook and Dan Klein to celebrate the artist's work. Not a true tile design but a most interesting medium for this fine artist's work.

Brown and buff encaustic tile, Minton & Co., 1866, 3 x 3

JS2013.527.11

No entry in my journal for this tile, perhaps I had no confidence in finding the other eight tiles to make a whole set.

Left: Encaustic tile, designed by John Pollard Seddon for Maw & Co., 1860–1880, 4¼ x 4¼

JS2013.527.12

This excellent and strong design was reproduced in large quantities with enormous colour ranges.

JS2013.527.7

This is one of my earliest English tiles. My great friend John Cox collects mostly 18th century Dutch and English tiles. We used to play rugby for the Harlequins together. In 1961 we won the Esher 7-a-side Rugby Cup; of such things friendships are made. Then I moved to collecting 19th-century English tiles. They were cheaper!

Hand-painted tile, designed by Edward Bawden for Carter & Co., 1930s, 5 x 5

JS2013.527.8

Richard Dennis, being the king of Victorian ceramics, jumped into the breach when they started to demolish the Poole Pottery Works Tea Rooms in 2000. The enterprise had been opened to the public in 1932. The restaurant was used as a factory canteen from 1946–1949 and the walls were covered in tiles. Richard Dennis and Graham Collyer at the last moment hacked the Poole tiles off the wall. I love Bawden's tile designs. He felt 'tile design' was rather beneath him! A minor battle in the field of decorative fine art. Fascinating!

Relief-moulded tile, Maw & Co., c.1890, 6 x 6

JS2013.527.5

One feels it was heavily inspired by a visit to the Alhambra in Granada. It would of course be immensely enriched by three more tiles to complete the necessary repeat. Try to imagine a dining room with walls covered with these tiles and then, as if by magic, lit by one hundred gloriously gilded wall brackets, each with four candles!

Relief-moulded tile, Maw & Co., c.1870, 6 x 6

JS2013.527.6

Bought from Tony Landau at the Barrett Street Supermarket, a good bunch of dealers. Gothic in style, just a pretty tile for a domestic interior.

Simulated mosaic tile, Maw & Co., c.1880, 7 x 7

JS2013.527.1

Excavations in Italy, particularly at Pompeii, often inspired tiles in the style of early Roman and Greek pavements.

Right: Sample encaustic tile for Palace of Westminster Project, Chris Cox for Craven Dunnill Jackfield Ltd, 2009, 6 x 6

JS2013.527.2

View of Chapel of Haddon Hall, designed by George H. Grundy for The Photo Decorated Tile Co. on a Pilkington blank, 1900–1909, 6 x 6

JS2013.527.3

Bought at a Phillips auction. These are quite rare and I am surprised they were not made in larger numbers. Much used on the continent for photos of the bereaved.

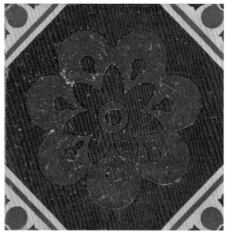

Encaustic tile, W. Godwin, 4¼ x 4¼

JS2013.527.13

Bought from John Stevens of Hammersmith Grove. Nice four-colour encaustic. Has anyone got the other three?

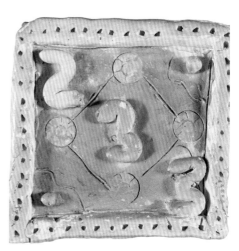

Handmade tile by John Scott's god-daughter, Ayumi, aged 8, 6 x 6

JS2013.527.4

Encaustic tile, W. Godwin, c.1870, 4⅛ x 4⅛

JS2013.527.14

A strong Gothic encaustic design that would be greatly enriched by three other tiles to make up the full picture. I have pressed the editors of *Glazed Expressions*, the excellent publication from TACS, to support a swaps corner to encourage the making up of incomplete pictures.

Relief-moulded tile, made by Pilkington for Tootall, Broadhurst, Lee, a textile company based on Oxford Street, Manchester, c.1900, 6 x 6

JS2013.527.15

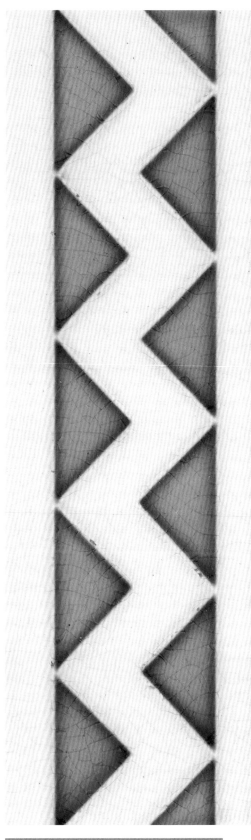

Relief-moulded border tile, Craven Dunnill & Co., c.1910, 6 x 2

JS2013.527.17

Bathrooms look better with borders.

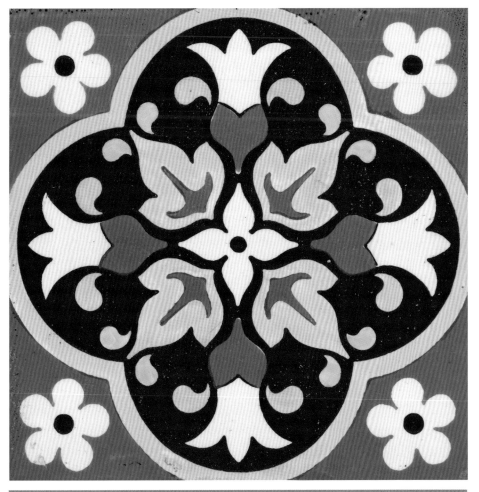

Block-printed and hand-coloured tile, designed by A.W.N. Pugin, Minton & Co., 1868–1900, 6 x 6

JS2013.527.16

An excellent design of timeless format and colour. Note the five petal florets in the corners … cinquefoil for the five wounds of Jesus Christ. Exquisite. For ecclesiastical use.

Tube-lined Art Deco tile, Pilkington, c.1930, 4 x 4

JS2013.527.18

Bought from Hans van Lemmen, President of the Tiles & Architectural Ceramics Society.

Tube-lined tile, Minton Hollins & Co., 1900–1920, 6 x 6

JS2013.527.20

No entry in my collecting journal; too tired or too lazy! On reflection it's perhaps rare – part of a jolly children's play room series.

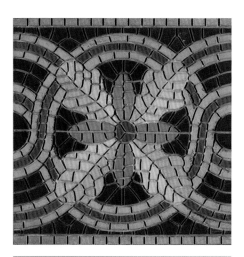

Simulated mosaic tile, 6 x 6

JS2013.527.19

Inspired by ancient Roman mosaic pavements.

Block-printed and hand-coloured tile, Minton Hollins & Co., 1875–1910, 6 x 6

JS2013.527.21

Very beautifully painted; it would be greatly improved as a border tile if there were two!

Transfer-printed aesthetic-style tile, c.1880, 6 x 6

JS2013.527.22

Heavy Japanese inspiration.

Encaustic border tile, Minton & Co., 6 x 1¾

JS2013.527.114

A rather charming and unusual border tile.

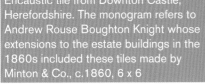

Encaustic tile from Downton Castle, Herefordshire. The monogram refers to Andrew Rouse Boughton Knight whose extensions to the estate buildings in the 1860s included these tiles made by Minton & Co., c.1860, 6 x 6

JS2013.527.23

I have not researched the owner of the initials ARBK. In fact I confess to being the antithesis of a proper tile collector. I simply bought what I liked and could afford. There is a vast amount of real research to be done on the technical details and I hope enthusiasts will rise to the challenge.

Above: Encaustic border tile, Minton & Co., 6 x 3

JS2013.527.107

Left: Encaustic tiles, c.1860, 4 x 4

JS2013.527.92, JS2013.527.99, JS2013.527.106, JS2013.527.113

Nice, but rather boring.

Relief-moulded majolica tiles, Craven Dunnill & Co., c.1880, 6 x 6

JS2013.527.95, JS2013.527.94, JS2013.527.93

Ideal for a cinema or dance hall. A fantastic decorative product which is almost timeless in its attraction. See the entrance to Brighton Museum.

Encaustic border tiles, possibly designed by A.W.N. Pugin, Minton & Co., c.1860, 6 x 6

JS2013.527.96, JS2013.527.97, JS2013.527.98

A greatly imposing and popular Minton tile. How the blue and white enrich it.

Far left: Encaustic tile, The Campbell Brick & Tile Co., 1875–1882, 6 x 6

JS2013.527.101

Note the curl of the leaves to create a three-dimensional effect, a 'Puginian' touch. First recognised by Clive Wainwright, the Pugin expert.

Left: Encaustic tile, Maw & Co., c.1860, 6 x 6

JS2013.527.102

Just a nice design, probably from the medieval.

JS2013.527.103, JS2013.527.104, JS2013.527.108, JS2013.527.105

Bought from Matt Townsend, a lovely tile.

JS2013.527.111, JS2013.527.109, JS2013.527.112, JS2013.527.110

Heavily inspired by the medieval.

JS2013.527.100

Bought from Leominster Restoration Centre, Ludlow Road. I tend to buy six encaustic tiles if the price is reasonable and I don't have the design. Michael Whiteway wanted me to cover a whole wall, floor to ceiling, with tiles, in which case they would not be at Jackfield Tile Museum but in my home.

Encaustic tile, Minton & Co., c.1870, 6 x 6

JS2013.527.138

Fleur-de-Lys, a commonly used symbol in encaustic tile design.

Encaustic tile, Maw & Co., 1860–1880, 6 x 6

JS2013.527.140

A strong design that I liked. One feels that this was designed by an artist who probably executed many designs for Maw & Co.

Encaustic border tile, Maw & Co., 1860 1880, 6 x 6

JS2013.527.139

A good quality design that just caught my eye.

Encaustic tile, Maw & Co., 1850–1852, 6 x 6

JS2013.527.142

Encaustic tile, Minton & Co., c.1860, 6 x 6

JS2013.527.141

This fish design is very common. Probably inspired by the early Christian fish symbols first noted in the Roman catacombs.

Encaustic tile, Chamberlain & Co., Worcester, 1840–1848, 6 x 6

JS2013.527.143

Just a good design.

Encaustic tile, The Campbell Brick &
Tile Co., 1875–1882, 6 x 6

JS2013.527.144

Very ordinary!

Above: Encaustic tiles, Minton & Co.,
1864, 6 x 6

**JS2013.527.146, JS2013.527.145, JS2013.527.147,
JS2013.527.148**

Survivors from the demolition of 16–34
Blenheim Crescent W11, Notting Hill
Housing Trust. I always bought polychrome
Minton encaustic tiles if they made a picture.
Now I have so many I am much more choosy.
However, the slight variation in style still
fascinates me.

Left: Transfer-print of Oxford Cathedral
from a series of Cathedrals designed by
L.T. Swetnam, Minton China Works,
c.1860, 6 x 6

JS2013.527.149

Bought at a Salvo (architectural salvage)
Fair at Knebworth. View of the back
probably from the Old Garden of Corpus
Christi College, sold to Christ Church many
years ago, probably 'for a song'! I was at
Corpus Christi College for three years from
1957–1959.

Encaustic tile, Maw & Co., c.1880, 6 x 6

JS2013.527.150

I always do enjoy finding multicoloured encaustic tiles. They require a dexterous hand to make – eight colours are rare. In the early days dealers did not count the colours. Now they repeat my comments back to me and charge me more, so keep your mouth shut! But that's boring and lacks conviviality, which is part of the fun and makes 'tile people' such a jolly lot.

Encaustic tile, Craven Dunnill & Co., 5 x 5

JS2013.527.152

Heavily inspired by the medieval. A gift from Andy Tilbrook, a great friend from 40 years back; he drives some 1,000 miles a week covering county sales in the hope of finding a sleeper (a mis-catalogued masterpiece!). It's all now fearfully competitive.

Encaustic tile, 6 x 6

JS2013.527.153

Bought from Adrian Grater, Ground Floor, Vernon Arcade, Portobello Road. A delightful man of great modesty who was a renowned ballet dancer in his youth. He is always very modest in his pricing. This glorious encaustic is a stylised Crown of Thorns.

Above: Encaustic tile, Minton & Co., 1889, 6 x 6

JS2013.527.154

A very striking tile.

Right: Encaustic tile, W. Godwin, 1851–1900, 6 diameter

JS2013.527.151

From Malcolm Fletcher of Birmingham. Malcolm has a very sharp eye for buildings just before the ball and chain arrives! Godwin were supreme in execution and design.

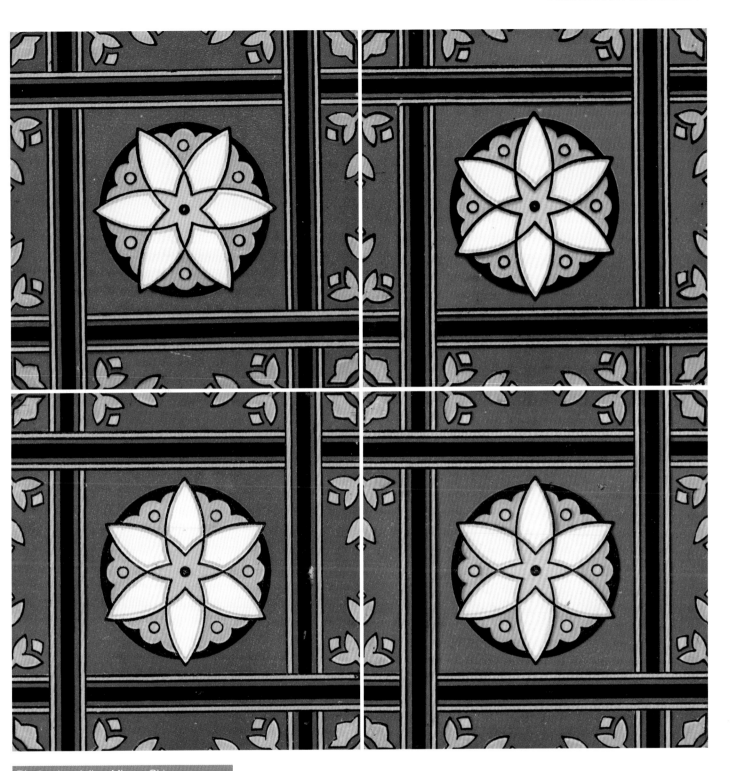

Block-printed tiles, Minton China
Works, 1868–1900, 6 x 6

**JS2013.527.159, JS2013.527.158, JS2013.527.157,
JS2013.527.160**

A 'Dresseresque' type of design. One
must be very careful not to ascribe to
dear Dr Dresser anything remotely like
his Studio Design. Efforts to magnify
the standing of one's collection in order
to make advantageous swaps must be
strongly resisted.

Glazed encaustic tile, designed by John Pollard Seddon, Maw & Co., 5½ x 5½

JS2013.527.155

A very rare, beautiful tile of immaculate form and rich honey colour; I enjoy the overlap of the flower stems.

Encaustic tile, W. Godwin, c.1840, 5 x 5

JS2013.527.156

Richard Coeur de Lion joins in a Crusade with Saladin. I like these very English images.

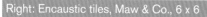

Right: Encaustic tiles, Maw & Co., 6 x 6

JS2013.527.168, JS2013.527.165, JS2013.527.166, JS2013.527.167

Akin to a kaleidoscope, made up almost exclusively of quatrefoils. It is amazing that such a complex visual conundrum can be created by quatrefoil dots to amuse the eye. I am lucky to have a large panel which enhances the aspect of this wonderful picture. Designed by John Pollard Seddon.

Opposite: Encaustic tiles, Minton & Co., 6 x 6

JS2013.527.164, JS2013.527.162, JS2013.527.163, JS2013.527.161

It's nice to identify the designer for a number of reasons: a) it enhances the collection b) it increases 'swapping power' and c) it increases the value. I have always tried to encourage TACS to have a 'swaps' page. I have considered the same endeavour with the Glass Circle but they feel this is too much like trading and against their aesthetic standing! Of course one can always use the Auction Rooms.

Right: Encaustic tiles, possibly made by Minton & Co., 6 x 6

JS2013.527.169, JS2013.527.170, JS2013.527.171, JS2013.527.172

The picture is modestly improved with four tiles together.

Left: Encaustic tiles, Minton & Co., c.1860, 6 x 6

JS2013.527.173, JS2013.527.175, JS2013.527.174, JS2013.527.176

It is extraordinary and delightful that such simple forms – trefoils, quatrefoils & multi-foils – can be arranged to make thousands of designs; such that the eye is never bored.

Encaustic tile, Maw & Co., 6 x 6

JS2013.527.354

A very strong design and greatly satisfying on the eye; rich with religious significance. This was illustrated in *The Building News*, 22 August 1873. Designed by John Pollard Seddon.

Hand-painted tile, designed by Truda Carter for Carter & Co., 1950s, 6 x 6

JS2013.527.315

The black field was very appealing and I adore the light touch of the painter. Carter tiles are almost always attractive as they choose excellent artists.

Encaustic tile, The Campbell Brick & Tile Co., 1875–1882, 6 x 6

JS2013.527.313

Encaustic tile, Robert Minton Taylor & Co., 1871–1874, 6 x 6

JS2013.527.314

Tube-lined tile, Malkin Tiles Ltd, c.1902, 6 x 6

JS2013.527.311

One benefit enjoyed by an aged collector – one learns when something is rare. I've never seen one in light and dark blue, pink and yellow before!

JS2013.527.309

These are vaguely Art Nouveau in style – glazed majolica; they must have been designed by someone as they have a strong 'designed' look. Not a favourite of mine, but interesting. I hope a visitor will add more knowledge and information on this and all my tiles.

Left: Relief-moulded, Maw & Co., 6 x 6

JS2013.527.312

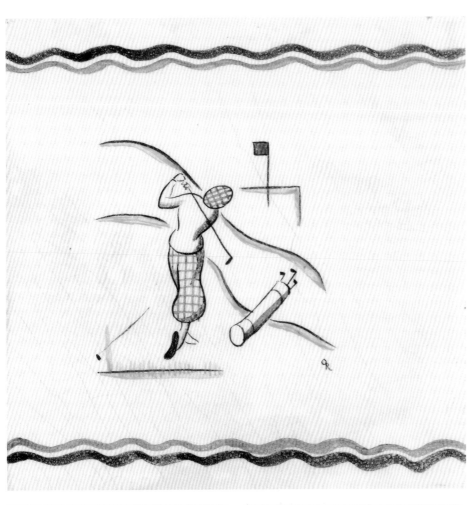

Above: Relief-moulded majolica tile, Minton & Co., 6 x 6

JS2013.527.307

These tiles were always top quality designs and never sloppy, the relief glaze always sparkled and polychrome is never boring. The enormous range of designs means that I am often lost in recollecting whether I already have an identical one. So, I may have duplicates, not counting varied 'colourways'. One must always remember that the tile industry was very competitive and all of the many companies were aiming to make a profit. This tile was used on the staircase at Minton Hollins factory.

Above: Part of the 'Sporting' series, designed by Thea Bridges, Packard & Ord on an H. & G. Thynne blank, 1948, 6 x 6

JS2013.527.310

Particularly charming and, although figurative, it is a most 'tiley' product. Gloriously crisp and although it could be rendered in pen and ink or watercolour it has a particular delight as a tile.

Left: Relief-moulded majolica tile, Minton & Co., 6 x 6

JS2013.527.305

A great example of the high design achievement of Victorian tiles with most fitting colourways. My three collecting journals list the tiles by date of purchase. The corresponding date sticker on the back of each tile sometimes falls off and then I am lost. The date on the sticker is the only way of knowing when it was bought, how much etc etc. This has been utterly infuriating. The loss of my stickers has caused me enormous grief.

Relief-moulded majolica tile, Minton & Co.,
6 x 6

JS2013.527.308

A very attractive, rich polychrome
'Dresseresque' majolica border tile. The
colours were most carefully chosen to
create a beautiful product. It is as beautiful a
border as you could dream of.

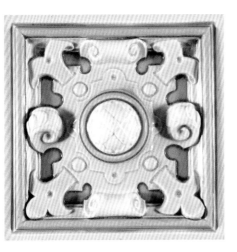

Relief-moulded tile, Wedgwood, 6 x 6

JS2013.527.306

In high relief and a very unusual design, similar to Royal Baths in Harrogate.

Transfer-printed and hand-painted tile, Copeland, 8 x 8

JS2013.527.301

This is a floreated, Gothic-inspired design. The trefoil and quatrefoil designs are constantly incorporated in Victorian tiles to evoke thoughts of the Holy Trinity and the four Gospels. The pink, light green and white are a delicious mélange, far from a sombre cloister.

Relief-moulded, Minton Hollins, 8 x 8

JS2013.527.302

The wave border, leaves, stems and flowers create, with a little imagination, a grandiose border. Imagine sitting in a candle-lit drawing room. The chair rail is below a row of these tiles around the entire room. Forget the Amber Room in St Petersburg!

Relief-moulded, Minton & Co., 1862, 6 x 6

JS2013.527.303

A Christmas present from my dear friend Andy Tilbrook. Latterly he shared a shop in the Halkin Arcade with Dan Klein. The shop was highly convenient for me when I worked for McKay Securities. It was a true Mecca for the growing number of collectors and dealers in Arts & Crafts, Art Nouveau, Art Deco, Gothic Revival etc. Some would assert this to be by C.F.A. Voysey but it lacks the sharpness of Voysey – too pretty pretty!!

Right: Relief-moulded tile, Minton & Co., 6 x 6

JS2013.527.304

Paid too much on basis it was C.F.A. Voysey. A very pretty tile in striking colours but it is not quite good enough. It is rare. At least I can be sure of that, having been collecting for over 50 years.

Border tile, Craven Dunnill & Co., 6 x 1

JS2013.527.375

To my mind this exemplifies the care and charm that was always at the fore in 19th- and early 20th-century decoration. How more satisfying to the eye is a large area of tiling edged with a neat border like this?

Hand-painted over-glaze tile designed by John Pearson on Maw & Co. blank, c.1905, 3 x 3

JS2013.527.355

Pearson was a prolific designer of tiles and stained glass.

Relief-moulded tile designed by Rafael Bordalo Pinheiro, Fabrica de Fainças das Caldas da Rainha, Portugal, 1905, 7½ x 7½

JS2013.527.377

Irritatingly expensive as there is a slice off the right side, possibly to fit it into a shop front. It is very rare and although I normally buy only British tiles this was so wonderful that I had to have it. It's as if Rafael Bordalo has seen William De Morgan and said, in Portuguese of course, 'I can do better'. Well … what do you think? You must visit Oporto to see glorious tile work. The lustrous influence of Moorish ceramics is a delight.

Left: Glazed encaustic tile, 6 x 6

JS2013.527.363

Only one of these, curse it. From Matt Townsend, who was a fabulous source of tiles in the late 70s. Those were great tile-buying times as there was a boom in property development – hence much demolition. Builders learned they could get 50p from Matt for a tile and thus spent much of their time saving tiles to sell instead of getting on with their jobs! I was able to buy encaustic tiles for £1. Matt then realised that painted tiles were more valuable and so he started collecting William De Morgan. A good thing never lasts forever!

Relief-moulded tile, Minton Hollins, 8 x 8

JS2013.527.299

Multi-foil floral sprays and gilded 'chain' squares in relief. A rare and beautiful secular tile of exquisite design.

Relief-moulded tile, Minton & Co., 8 x 8

JS2013.527.300

Exhibited by Jeremy Cooper in his Minton Majolica Exhibition. Jeremy had a huge gallery near the British Museum and was one of the major dealers in British Decorative Art. This superbly executed tile with rich polychrome patterns in relief would make a superb border with a nautical touch.

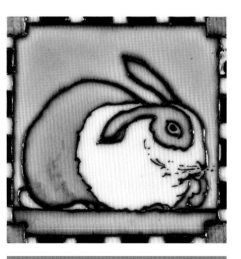

Tube-lined tile, designed by Edmund Kent, Pilkington's Tile & Pottery Co. Ltd, 1932, 4 x 4

JS2013.527.356

I remember feeling rather strongly that this was a high price; but it was very finely made with a nice, raised border. Moreover, whilst representational – a mere rabbit – the image is most successful. I liked it very much.

Right: Border tile, Craven Dunnill & Co., 6 x 1

JS2013.527.374

Just a nice 1920/30s border tile.

Hand-painted tile, part of the 'Fishermen'
series designed by Sylvia Packard, Packard
& Ord, on Pilkington blank, 1946, 6 x 6

JS2013.527.365

A strange image of a man kitted out in all
the clothing and accoutrements of an upper
class country gentleman – top hat, spats,
fishing rod – giving full attention to fixing a
dry fly for trout fishing.

Screen-printed tile designed by Otto
Eckmann, Villeroy & Boch, Mettlach, pre-
1899, 6 x 6

JS2013.527.364

Bought at the annual TACS Tile Fair
at St Jude's Church Hall, Mapperley,
Nottingham. This is a delightful occasion
that all tile lovers should attend. Mike Blood
is invariably in attendance to feed the
company or show his superb tile collection,
or both.

Transfer-printed and hand-painted tile,
Minton Hollins & Co., 1875–1910, 6 x 6

JS2013.527.361

Very beautiful gold lustre tile that needs four
more tiles to complete the picture. A.W.N.
Pugin-inspired, with multi-foil corners.
Frequently the serious tile collector is utterly
frustrated by the dealer who (for many
reasons, including finance or sheer weight)
'just buys one'. They never tell you where the
rest can be found!

Screen-printed outline, hand-coloured tile,
E. Pritchard for Dorincourt Industries on a
Carter blank, post-1959, 6 x 6

JS2013.527.362

The TACS Tile Fair is an annual event organised
by the Tiles & Architectural Ceramics Society
and is enormous fun. It's a kind of Bring &
Buy sale; all the members are friendly, full
of bonhomie and shared enthusiasm for …
TILES. Everything is most reasonably priced
which adds to the activity. I greatly love
and admire TACS and my desire is that the
computer record of my collection will inspire
others to donate tiles to fill gaps. Over time,
my mistakes will be corrected and knowledge
will be expanded. The aim should be to create,
preserve and enhance the greatest British tile
collection in the world. Not mine!

Hand-painted tile from 'The Chase' series, designed by Edward Bawden for Carter & Co., 1930s, 6 x 6

JS2013.527.366

'Coarse' Fishing – after pike with a plug.

Hand-painted tile from 'The Chase' series, designed by Edward Bawden for Carter & Co., 1930s, 5 x 5

JS2013.527.357

Very posh lady blowing horn for the chase. I had a lovely contrasting tile of a coarse fisherman with a 'cor blimey' hat. A fascinating image of the English class system – coarse fishing with plug lure for pike, upper-class lady in silk shirt and upper-crust top hat!

Hand-painted tile from the 'Sporting' series, designed by Edward Bawden for Carter & Co., c.1935, 5 x 5

JS2013.527.358

I am always much amused that Bawden did not like to have it known that he designed tiles! This is an example of the conflict between 'Fine' and 'Decorative' Art. Being a lover of Victorian decorative art I can laugh at this. A well-known glass artist once told me he was now into 'glass sculpture'. Fine Art sells at a premium above mere craftware.

Dust-pressed encaustic tile, Malkin Edge & Co., 6 x 6

JS2013.527.360

This is a masterpiece of design. It is the glaring and arresting quality and strength of many Victorian tiles which has so attracted me to this field. Happily I have four of these, 40 would be better, if space and availability allowed. Probably Dresser or Pugin.

Relief-moulded tile, Maw & Co., 6 x 6

JS2013.527.359

Highly dramatic in both colour and image, the glory of this tile is probably only fully achieved on a wall. The expanse of tiles then exposes the tile lover to a visual feast. Collectors should strive to assemble tiles to reveal the full image. This often requires 4, 9, 16 or even 25 tiles.

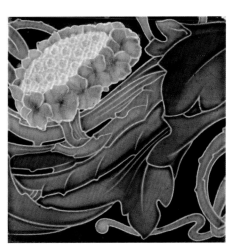

Tube-lined Art Nouveau tile, Minton & Co., 6 x 6

JS2013.527.376

I maintain there is very little Art Nouveau in Britain. The swirling whiplash images I feel were a bit too much for our rather straightlaced taste. However this one is a cracker with colour and swerve. Oh that there were more to make a gorgeous picture!

Portrait of Tuari Netana, photographic tile by George Cartlidge for Sherwin & Cotton, c.1890, 6 x 9

JS2013.527.373

Slightly in relief and richly glazed to create a striking effect, this shows one of four Maori subjects. One forgets that the purpose of tiles like other commodities was to make money. Innovation was as important in the late 19th century as fashion is today. These images must have been very popular as New Zealand was substantially unknown. Westbourne Grove was a great hunting ground for antiques. Now it's all high fashion.

Tube-lined Art Nouveau tile, Minton & Co., 6 x 6

JS2013.527.371

I bought this because of its Art Nouveau 'twirly whirly' aspect. Interesting how the leaves are folded over to make a three-dimensional effect; perhaps Pugin's influence lives on.

Hand-painted tile, Pilkington's Tiles Ltd, 1953, 6 x 6

JS2013.527.372

Bought from Paddy Frost, an excellent specialist tile dealer in Antiquarius – a fine Antiques Emporium in the King's Road, Chelsea. Now another clothes shop.

JS2013.527.367

A number of charming scenes of Poole and its surroundings were made – I presume as giftware, extolling the various activities available to tourists. Make friends with a dealer if you want to make progress.

JS2013.527.370

The whole artistic character of the London Underground was masterminded by Frank Pick. It was a fabulous enterprise combining practicalities and top quality designers and architects. The tiles were designed by Stabler and have a creamy finish and character. This tile illustrates the HQ of London Transport; other images were appropriate to the location. It is a great shame there are very few of Stabler's little jewels remaining. St Paul's has a few that are worth visiting. Some stations have been modernised in different ways. Sir Eduardo Paolozzi has designed a fabulous modern tile extravaganza at Tottenham Court Road.

JS2013.527.368

These are of course representational and the proper medium for these are watercolours. Maxwell was fed up with collectors allowing his work to fade by excessive exposure to light. He persuaded Doulton to glaze his work. Hence, a number are tiles. I have broken my rule. Frankly they are watercolour images and not 'tiley'. But I like them. They were also evocative of Roland Hilder – loved by me from 1948.

Encaustic tile, Minton & Co., 4¼ x 4¼

JS2013.527.426

Good design. It'd be nice to get another three!

Encaustic tile panel, W. Godwin, 9 x 9

JS2013.527.413

A good design.

Line-impressed tile, 4¼ x 4¼

JS2013.527.428

Richard Coeur de Lion.

Above: Transfer-printed and hand-painted tile, designed by A.W.N. Pugin, Minton & Co., c.1870, 6 x 6

JS2013.527.369

Thirty years ago I catalogued this in my book, 'rather silly looking snowdrops – rather post-Pugin looking!'. Now I think I would upgrade my view and consider it a superior design and good colour choice. The black field enhances the images and the borders are entrancing to the eye and never boring. Bought from Eddie Evans of Prenton Antiques, Birkenhead. An ex-butcher, Eddie was a fabulous and famed dealer often visited by Jonathan Horne, the first President of Guild of Antique Dealers.

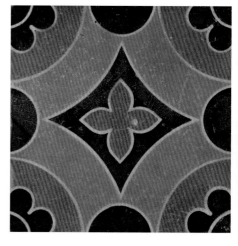

Encaustic tile, Minton & Co., 1864, 4¼ x 4¼

JS2013.527.429

Surprisingly bold and dramatic in colour and form. Having four would make for a stunning design.

Left: Intaglio-moulded and brown-glazed tile, Minton Hollins & Co., c.1860, 5⅞ x 5⅞

JS2013.527.415

I must have seen at least twenty variants. This fish design is very common. Probably inspired by the early Christian fish symbols first noted in the Roman catacombs.

Block-printed gold lustre tile, Minton
Hollins & Co., 8 x 8

JS2013.527.414

An exquisite tile. I always imagine my
Valhalla decorated with these tiles and lit by
candles.

Encaustic tile, 5⅞ x 5⅞

JS2013.527.416

Very Christian; all quatrefoils and trefoils.

Encaustic tile, Chamberlain & Co.,
1840–1848, 6 x 6

JS2013.527.419

Pretty ordinary. I would not buy it today!

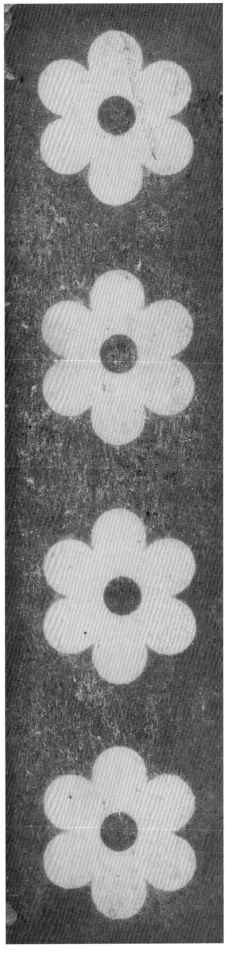

Encaustic border tile, 6½ x 1½

JS2013.527.427

Encaustic tile, Chamberlain & Co.,
1840–1848, 6 x 6

JS2013.527.420

Unusual finely wrought encaustic with a
delicate design.

Transfer-printed tile, designed by John
Windsor Bradburn, Minton Hollins & Co.,
4¼ x 4¼

JS2013.527.425

Very strong design.

Encaustic tiles, W. Godwin, 5¼ x 5¼

JS2013.527.422, JS2013.527.421, JS2013.527.424,
JS2013.527.423

Inspired by medieval designs, with a
distressed finish. A very lucky buy from
Michael Whiteway.

Encaustic border tile, 8½ x 1½

JS2013.527.430

Encaustic tile, Minton & Co., c.1865, 6 x 6

JS2013.527.417

Encaustic tile, Chamberlain & Co., 1840–1848, 6 x 6

JS2013.527.418

Encaustic tile, designed by A.W.N. Pugin, Minton & Co., 1868, 6 x 6

JS2013.527.431

Designed by A.W.N. Pugin, or rather more accurately, inspired by the medieval and sharpened up for his friend, Sir Herbert Minton. Bought from a nice lady with a dog on the main road outside Hungerford.

Tube-lined Art Nouveau tile, 6 x 6

JS2013.527.432

Very rare, very Art Nouveau.

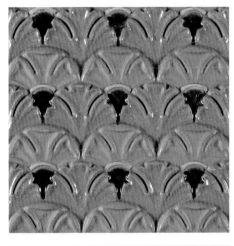

Relief-moulded tile, designed by John Pollard Seddon, Maw & Co., c.1870, 6 x 6

JS2013.527.434

A very beautiful architectural tile.

Glazed encaustic, W. Godwin, 6 x 6

JS2013.527.433

Bought at the annual TACS Fair. Tiles are never highly priced and I always buy about six. I think this is a six-colour tile which I like as Chris Cox has taught me they are much harder to make. Some collectors will only collect perfect items. I don't mind if I like it but I expect a reduction in price! A lovely enthralling design often seen in wide variety of colourways.

Left: Encaustic tile, designed by John Pollard Seddon, Maw & Co., 6 x 5

JS2013.527.437

Encaustic tile, Maw & Co., 4 x 4

JS2013.527.438

My modern sticky labels are of such poor quality they dry and fall off frequently. In contrast, Victorian stickers on ancient discoveries from Egypt etc. still stay on. Oh, the modern world is so frustrating!

Relief-moulded tile, Minton & Co., 6 x 6

JS2013.527.435

I paid far too much but it was so pretty and it had been a long drive. And if I was a reasonably serious collector I must take note that the market has gone up. So if I want to stay in the market and if I can afford it, I must pay more! What a glorious chair rail for a children's room or a conservatory. As with much in life a rich imagination can help a lot! If you have a huge collection, a wildly high price can be 'averaged' over the whole lot for a fractional increase on say 2,000 tiles! It's the really big fish that 'gets away' that you truly regret.

Encaustic tiles, designed by John Pollard Seddon, Maw & Co., 6 x 6

JS2013.527.436, JS2013.527.439

John Pollard Seddon designed a lot for Maw & Co. and this is an excellent heavily religious Gothic image. Note the strong Christian signage, trefoils for the Holy Trinity and quatrefoils for the four Holy Gospels.

Designed by William Wise for Minton & Co., 6 x 6

JS2013.527.440

One feels this is more of a watercolour or oil painting image and I agree. However, William Wise painted beautiful animals for Minton – farmyard scenes of great quality and rare panache.

Hand-painted tile, William De Morgan, on a Maw & Co. blank, 6 x 6

JS2013.527.442

Hand-painted tile, William De Morgan on an Architectural Pottery Co. blank, 6 x 6

JS2013.527.441

Richard Myers wrote a most useful book on Morris tiles. The greatest collector of William De Morgan tiles was Jon Catleugh. His collection has been dispersed by auction etc. It is unlikely ever to be surpassed. He was most generous with his advice and a great supporter of the William De Morgan Foundation.

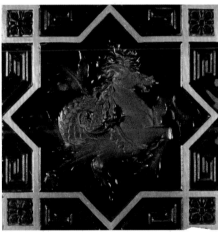

Relief-moulded tile, Minton & Co., 6 x 6

JS2013.527.443

A very fine image in relief, the horse is unglazed to stand out so strikingly with the gold.

Left: An example of Hardstone or Pietra Dura, inlaid semi-precious stone tile, 6⅝ x 4½

JS2013.527.444

Relief-moulded tiles, Minton & Co., 6 x 6

JS2013.527.445, JS2013.527.446

Dark field with very bright majolica creates a glorious effect. I have seen probably twenty colour variants of this tile, which is such a good tile design that it would have been popular for many areas of tiling. Probably John Seddon.

Photographic tile showing Windsor Castle by George Grundy for The Photo Decorated Tile Co. on a Pilkington blank, c.1900, 6 x 6

JS2013.527.447

Such mementos of tourist attractions seem much more useful (many were made as teapot stands) and attractive than the throwaway geegaws of the modern world.

Designed by Jonathan Chiswell Jones, 2010, 5¾ x 5¾

JS2013.527.449

Modern, exquisite, rich polychrome lustre tile made c.2010 by Jonathan Chiswell Jones. I first met Jonathan when he was selling his ceramics through Bonhams Auctioneers on Bond Street. He has mastered the art of lustre and has definitely surpassed William De Morgan. I remember he came for lunch at my home and I enjoyed a little joke. Aligning a triple lustre William De Morgan plate next to one of his lustre chargers I exclaimed, 'you're better than William De Morgan but I do think you should wipe the oil off yours'. So lustrous are his designs that they shine as if coated in oil. Perhaps William De Morgan is just different.

Photographic tile by George Grundy for The Photo Decorated Tile Co. on a Pilkington blank, c.1900, 6 x 6

JS2013.527.448

Charming scene. It's the kind of image that seems more appropriate as a drawing, watercolour or oil painting. Nevertheless it demonstrates decoration of a most enduring form.

Encaustic tile, Minton & Co., 6 x 6

JS2013.527.462

Opposite: Encaustic tiles, designed by E.W. Pugin, Minton & Co., c.1870, 6 x 6

JS2013.527.451

Given to me by Dom Bede Millard of The Grange, Ramsgate. Built by A.W.N. Pugin and completed by his son E.W. Pugin.

Encaustic tile, Minton & Co., 6 x 6

JS2013.527.460

Encaustic tile, E. Smith & Co., Coalville, 6 x 6

JS2013.527.458

Encaustic tiles, W. Godwin, 6 x 6

JS2013.527.459, JS2013.527.461

Relief-moulded tiles, Maw & Co., 6¾ x 12¾

JS2013.527.450

The play of light on the raised surface of majolica tiles can be outstandingly attractive.

Encaustic tile, Godwin & Hewitt, c.1905, 6 x 6

JS2013.527.456

Left: Encaustic tiles, Minton & Co., 1864, 6 x 6

JS2013.527.453, JS2013.527.454, JS2013.527.455, JS2013.527.452

Right: Encaustic tiles, Steele & Wood, Minton & Co., 4¼ x 4¼

JS2013.527.463, JS2013.527.464, JS2013.527.465, JS2013.527.466

Just an attractive pattern which is enriched by having four tiles that open up a series of patterns. The eye is very unlikely to be bored.

Encaustic tile, Minton & Co., 1880, 6 x 6

JS2013.527.457

Encaustic tiles, Minton & Co., 6 x 6

JS2013.527.470, JS2013.527.468, JS2013.527.469, JS2013.527.467

Note how the increase in colour – black, blue, red and fawn – adds distinction. But often eight colours, though impressive and more difficult to execute, does not increase the overall effect commensurately.

Left: Transfer-printed and hand-painted tiles, designed by A.W.N. Pugin, Minton & Co., 6 x 6

JS2013.527.474, JS2013.527.473, JS2013.527.472, JS2013.527.471

I suspect this design, being a strong and popular one, continued to be made well after his death.

Encaustic tile, W. Godwin, 6 x 6

JS2013.527.479

Encaustic tiles, Maw & Co., 6 x 6

**JS2013.527.477, JS2013.527.476, JS2013.527.478,
JS2013.527.475**

Unusual. Naturally like all collectors I seek
the unusual.

Encaustic tile, W. Godwin, 6 x 6

JS2013.527.480

Needs another three to make up the picture.

Encaustic border tile, Minton & Co., 6 x 6

JS2013.527.481

Encaustic tile, Architectural Pottery Co.,
6 x 6

JS2013.527.482

Encaustic tile, Minton & Co., 6 x 6

JS2013.527.489

Left: Encaustic tiles, St George's Tile Works, 6 x 6

JS2013.527.483, JS2013.527.484, JS2013.527.485, JS2013.527.486

Relief-moulded tiles, Minton Hollins & Co., 6 x 6

JS2013.527.487, JS2013.527.488

From a High Altar. Think of Jesus.

Right: Encaustic tile, Maw & Co., 6 x 4

JS2013.527.490

Superb vertical border tile. The *Journal of Decorative Art, Volume III* from 1887 describes the mode of construction of these tiles.

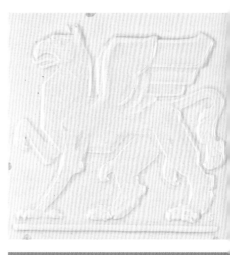

Relief-moulded tile, designed by Harold Stabler for the London Underground, Carter & Co., 1930s, 6 x 6

JS2013.527.511

The Underground was masterminded by an unsung hero, Frank Pick. Almost everything was carefully selected and made with zip, zest and panache. Stabler designed individual designs for almost all stations; they have now been ripped out by the modernizers. Mike Ashcroft of Heritage of London Underground has generously given more tiles to Ironbridge. Many thanks. Encourage others to give tiles under threat.

Encaustic tiles, Minton & Co., 1864, 6 x 6

JS2013.527.494, JS2013.527.491, JS2013.527.492, JS2013.527.493

Salvaged from the Notting Hill Housing Trust, 16–34 Blenheim Crescent, London W11.

Encaustic tile, monogram for John Talbot, Earl of Shrewsbury, designed by A.W.N. Pugin, Minton & Co., 1860, 6 x 6

JS2013.527.509

Encaustic tile, Minton & Co., 6 x 6

JS2013.527.510

Salvaged from Osborne House. Bought from Don Kelly, Vernon Arcade, Portobello Road. Very nice piece of calligraphic encaustic work.

Encaustic tile, Minton & Co., 6 x 6

JS2013.527.512

I adore this one – designed by A.W.N. Pugin. I feel like looking for a No. 2 house so that I can fix this delectable numeral upon its portal and so enjoy it on every entry. I wax lyrical because this is a masterpiece of typography.

Left: Encaustic tiles relating to John Talbot, 16th Earl of Shrewsbury, designed by A.W.N. Pugin, Minton & Co., 6 x 6

JS2013.527.523, JS2013.527.513

I always thought this was part of the Grosvenor coat of arms, both families having abundant rolling acres of farm land. Generously given by Sister Kyran of St Mary's Convent, Hunters Road, Birmingham.

Right: Encaustic tiles, possibly designed by Christopher Dresser, Minton & Co., 6 x 6

JS2013.527.514, JS2013.527.516

Everyone now says these are by Dr Christopher Dresser and raises the price accordingly. I know of no proof. But the design is of sumptuous intricacy. I'll never forget the vendor lady saying, 'I'll be back next week with 10 more'. She never came back!

Encaustic tile, 6 x 6

JS2013.527.515

Encaustic tile, Minton & Co., 6 x 6

JS2013.527.517

Very early Minton; failures in the blunging machine resulted in air pockets which have defaced the front of the tile. I am cursing those who hate faults.

Encaustic tile, W. Godwin, 6 x 6

JS2013.527.518

This tile has worn … charmingly! If polished as I saw the ladies polishing the tiles in the parish church in Mold, then the reflections of candlelight would be celestial, though slippery!

Encaustic tile, W. Godwin, 6 x 6

JS2013.527.519

From a swap with my friend Bob Smith at the TACS annual tile fest at Nottingham. Enormously thick – there's an example at Sunninghill Church, Oxford. Designed by John Pollard Seddon.

Encaustic tile, 6 x 6

JS2013.527.522

From a swap with my friend Bob Smith at the TACS annual tile fest at Nottingham. Enormously thick – there's an example at Sunninghill Church, Oxford. By John Pollard Seddon.

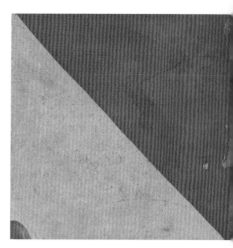

Encaustic tile, Maw & Co., 1850–1852, 6 x 6

JS2013.527.521

Encaustic tile, Minton & Co., 1863, 6 x 6

JS2013.527.520

Very fine image inspired by antiquity.

Transfer-printed tile, 5½ x 8½

JS2013.527.527

A gift from Keith Horie.

Encaustic tile, Robert Minton Taylor, 4 x 4

JS2013.527.524

Breathtaking execution, like enamelling.

Flemish encaustic tile, 16th century, 5½ x 5½

JS2013.527.528

Relief-moulded tile, designed by C.F.A. Voysey as a self-portrait depicting the devil, J.C. Edwards (Ruabon), c.1900, 6 x 6

JS2013.527.526

Voysey's entire *oeuvre* is imbued with the gentle country idylls, whether it be architecture, wood or metal work, watercolours, textiles or furniture. His whole life was the very antithesis of the devil. He died sadly in relative poverty painting exquisite watercolours of landscapes and flowers which now make enormous sums.

Transfer-printed tile from the 'Farm' series, designed by William Wise, Minton & Co., 6 x 6

JS2013.527.529

William Wise – a master craftsman of rustic folk.

Encaustic tile, W. Godwin, 6 x 6

JS2013.527.597

Exquisitely made. The very highest quality of encaustics both in design and execution. In my Top Ten.

Left: Encaustic tile for Sandon Hall, Staffs, Chris Cox, Craven Dunnill Jackfield Ltd, 4 x 4

JS2013.527.525

A present to me from Chris Cox of Craven Dunnill Jackfield Ltd, being a 4¼ encaustic that he had made. Chris is the leader of a team now restoring the worn tiles in the Palace of Westminster. It's a job like painting the Forth Bridge! It is most welcome to see this ancient craft being so successfully rejuvenated. Note the colour shading like 'wireless cloisonné'.

Right: Encaustic tiles, Craven Dunnill & Co., 4¼ x 4¼

JS2013.527.590, JS2013.527.592, JS2013.527.591, JS2013.527.589

Very eye-catching.

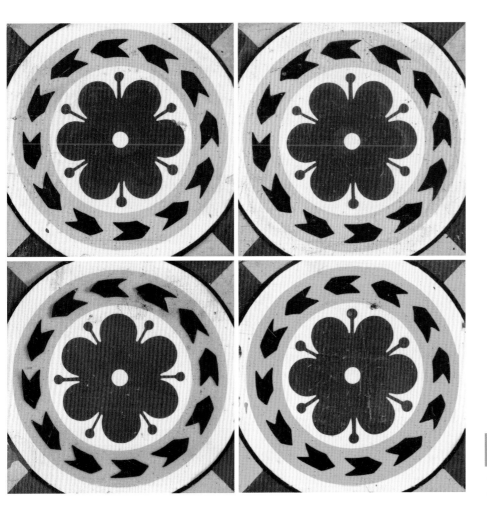

Left: Encaustic tiles, Minton Hollins & Co., 4¼ x 4¼

JS2013.527.594, JS2013.527.595, JS2013.527.596, JS2013.527.593

Right: Encaustic tiles, Maw & Co., 6 x 6

JS2013.527.600, JS2013.527.599, JS2013.527.601, JS2013.527.598

Floreated Gothic style bought from Bill Dickinson, Tudor House, 11 Tontine Hill, opposite the Iron Bridge.

Left: Encaustic tiles, W. Godwin, 6 x 6

JS2013.527.605, JS2013.527.604, JS2013.527.603, JS2013.527.602

Right: Encaustic tiles, possibly designed by A.W.N. Pugin, Minton & Co., 6 x 6

JS2013.527.607, JS2013.527.608, JS2013.527.606, JS2013.527.609

A very great design, again seen in varied colourways. Saved from 16–34 Blenheim Crescent, London W11.

Encaustic tiles, Minton & Co., 1871, 6 x 6

JS2013.527.613, JS2013.527.612, JS2013.527.611, JS2013.527.610

I feel this is my favourite tile especially in a picture made up of nine tiles. The joker is there as a figure of fun, or perhaps he is a Green Man – albeit black! Perhaps this is a Dresser joke. Enormously satisfying. The eye is never bored that gazes here.

Right: Encaustic tiles, Chamberlain & Co., 1840–1848, 6 x 6

JS2013.527.618, JS2013.527.620, JS2013.527.621, JS2013.527.619

Sixty-eight tiles that had never been laid were found in a house in Scotland.

Encaustic tile, Minton & Co., 7 x 7

JS2013.527.626

Left: Encaustic tiles, Chamberlain & Co., 1840–1848, 6 x 6

JS2013.527.614, JS2013.527.615, JS2013.527.617, JS2013.527.616

Sixty-eight tiles that had never been laid were found in a house in Scotland.

Encaustic tile, Minton & Co., 1871, 6 x 6

JS2013.527.622

Very exciting and quixotic black-field encaustic.

Right: Relief-moulded tiles, Maw & Co., 6 x 6

JS2013.527.629, JS2013.527.630, JS2013.527.628, JS2013.527.627

A very beautiful tile bought from Myriad Antiques. I bought three others to make a picture. The one tile usually stands alone.

Encaustic tiles, designed by A.W.N. Pugin, Minton & Co., 6 x 6

JS2013.527.633, JS2013.527.631, JS2013.527.634, JS2013.527.632

Well established A.W.N. Pugin design from Shepshed Church. This frequently appears with different colourways.

Left: Encaustic tile, Minton & Co., 6 x 6

JS2013.527.623

A very fine strong design. If not Dresser then someone of his calibre.

Encaustic tile, Craven Dunnill & Co., 7 x 7

JS2013.527.624

Encaustic tile, Craven Dunnill & Co., 6¾ x 6¾

JS2013.527.625

Left: Encaustic tiles, Minton Hollins & Co., 4 x 4

JS2013.527.635, JS2013.527.636, JS2013.527.637, JS2013.527.638

This is an outstanding design and one of my very favourites by Minton & Co. It must be by a top artist. Can you identify him or her?

Relief-moulded tiles, Minton Hollins & Co.,
4 x 4

**JS2013.527.647, JS2013.527.646, JS2013.527.639,
JS2013.527.644, JS2013.527.645, JS2013.527.643,
JS2013.527.642, JS2013.527.641, JS2013.527.640**

An exceptionally rich Minton Hollins splash
of Gothic brilliance. Note how ennobled the
whole image is made with nine or more tiles
instead of one!

Relief-moulded tile, Minton & Co., 7 x 7

JS2013.527.660

Very rare – no doubt from a 'titled' family.

Encaustic tiles, W. Godwin, 4 x 4

JS2013.527.648, JS2013.527.649, JS2013.527.650, JS2013.527.651

Good design.

Relief-moulded majolica tiles, Minton Hollins & Co., 4 x 4

JS2013.527.654, JS2013.527.655, JS2013.527.653, JS2013.527.652

Left: Relief-moulded tiles, Minton Hollins & Co., 4 x 4

JS2013.527.657, JS2013.527.656, JS2013.527.658, JS2013.527.659

Very rich polychrome tile from Somerset Maugham's house – The Old Vicarage, Saddleton Road, Whitstable.

Right: Relief-moulded majolica tiles, Minton Hollins & Co., 4 x 4

JS2013.527.664, JS2013.527.661, JS2013.527.663, JS2013.527.662

Very expensive but I find these small, four-inch tiles jewel-like in aspect.

JS2013.527.667, JS2013.527.665, JS2013.527.668, JS2013.527.666

A great design probably by Dr Christopher Dresser. Entrancing geometric design in a floreated Gothic style. In my Top Ten.

JS2013.527.672, JS2013.527.670, JS2013.527.671, JS2013.527.669

An excellent design.

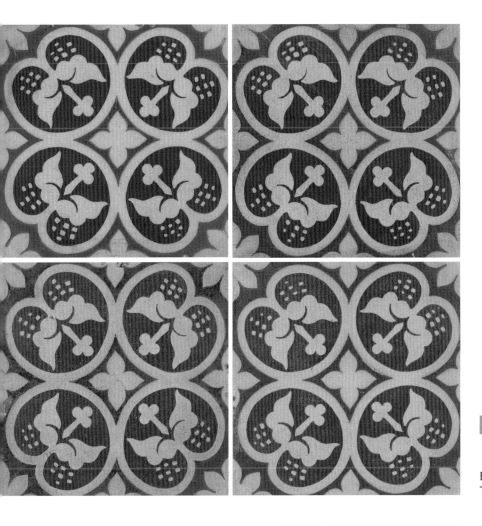

JS2013.527.676, JS2013.527.675, JS2013.527.673, JS2013.527.674

Excellent. Many colour ways. In my Top Twenty. Probably A.W.N. Pugin.

JS2013.527.678, JS2013.527.677, JS2013.527.679, JS2013.527.680

Also in my Top Twenty. Probably A.W.N. Pugin.

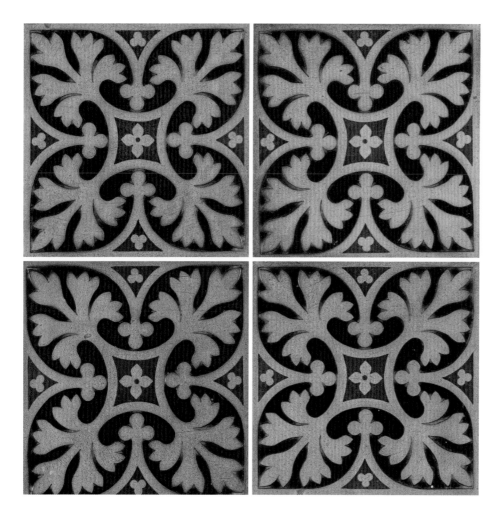

Left: Encaustic tiles, Minton & Co., c.1870, 6 x 6

JS2013.527.681, JS2013.527.683, JS2013.527.682, JS2013.527.684

Right: Encaustic tiles, Minton & Co., 6 x 6¾

JS2013.527.693, JS2013.527.694, JS2013.527.691, JS2013.527.692

Quite a busy design with Scottish spirit.

Encaustic tile, Minton & Co., 1871, 6 x 6

JS2013.527.685

Fascinating mélange of fantastical dragons
and wild beasts bought from Dickinsons
Antique Market in Ludlow.

**Left: Glazed encaustic tiles, W. Godwin,
6 x 6**

JS2013.527.689, JS2013.527.690, JS2013.527.688,
JS2013.527.687

This is an excellent tile design that I have
seen in at least 12 different colourways.
The corners seem like stylised ears of
corn which might be symbols of a rich
agricultural area.

Encaustic tile, Minton & Co., c.1860, 6 x 6

JS2013.527.686

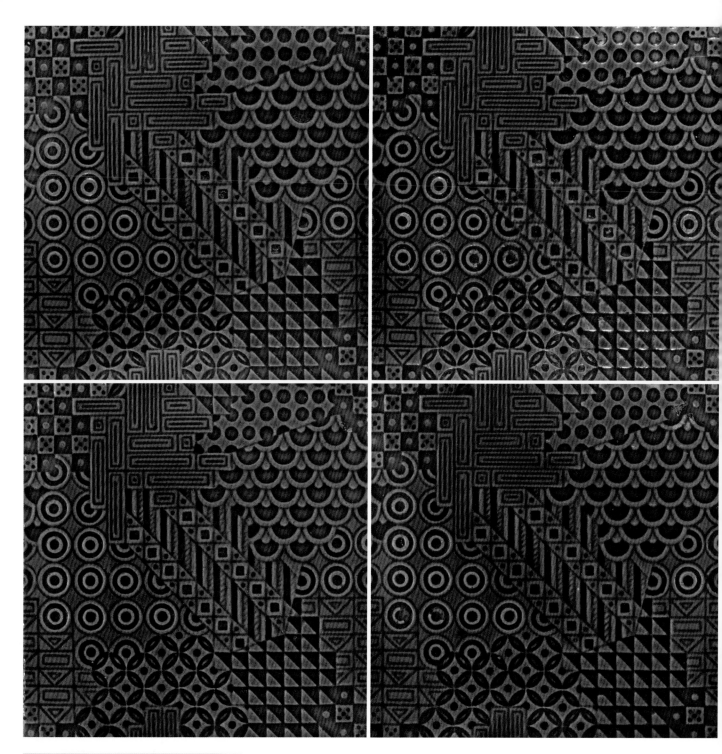

Relief-moulded tiles, W. Godwin, 6 x 6

JS2013.527.698, JS2013.527.697, JS2013.527.696, JS2013.527.695

I have never seen another tile of this type. One of the great fascinations of collecting tiles is to constantly discover new types. The enormous popularity of tiles and the vast number of factories account for this amazing profusion.

Transfer-printed tiles, 6 x 6

**JS2013.527.701, JS2013.527.702, JS2013.527.700,
JS2013.527.704, JS2013.527.699, JS2013.527.703**

This beautiful and complex pattern requires 16 tiles to reveal the image in its entirety. The likelihood of ever finding the missing tiles is so remote that I would like the conservator to fill the gap with photographs. The effort will be much rewarded.

Encaustic tile, Copeland and Garrett, 1837–1840, 6 x 6

JS2013.527.736

For a more interesting display I would place this alongside a differing colourway but with same design. What do you think? A beautiful rendering of the anthemion, the most inspiring flower of the Roman and Greek world.

Encaustic tile, Copeland and Garrett, 1837–1840, 6 x 6

JS2013.527.740

I have four of these bold and striking anthemion tiles in different colours and style.

Border tiles, designed by Christopher Dresser, Minton China Works, 6 x 6

JS2013.527.738, JS2013.527.737

Anthemion again.

Encaustic tile, Minton & Co., 6 x 6

JS2013.527.739

A good example of the need for another tile to complete a design.

Encaustic tile, Minton & Co., 6 x 6

JS2013.527.773

Quatrefoils and trefoils galore!

Encaustic tiles, designed by A.W.N. Pugin, Minton & Co., 1861, 6 x 6

JS2013.527.742, JS2013.527.741, JS2013.527.743, JS2013.527.744

A known Pugin design. Pugin persuaded Minton to enliven and enrich the standard buff and red Minton encaustics – blue being the most common addition.

Encaustic tiles, W. Godwin, 4 x 4

JS2013.527.747, JS2013.527.753, JS2013.527.748,
JS2013.527.752, JS2013.527.749, JS2013.527.751,
JS2013.527.750, JS2013.527.745, JS2013.527.746

A particularly excellent example of an encaustic design. You might consider this ecclesiastical with its trefoils and quatrefoils. However, the soft and luscious colours make one see such a floor as ideal for a conservatory. How much better in every respect is this image with nine tiles rather than one or even four, but how about 40 or 400! In my Top Ten.

Encaustic tile, Craven Dunnill & Co., 6 x 3

JS2013.527.754

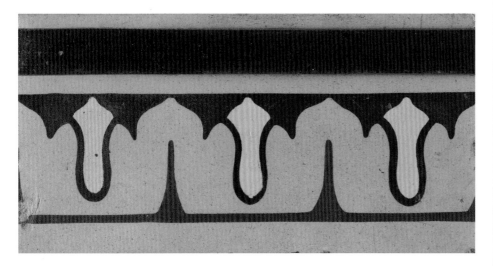

Encaustic tile, Minton & Co., 1862, 6 x 3

JS2013.527.755

Simple but fine, a modest four-colour encaustic.

Encaustic tile, Minton & Co., c.1840, 6 x 6

JS2013.527.774

Right: Encaustic tiles, Minton Hollins & Co., 2 x 6

JS2013.527.819, JS2013.527.775

From St Catherine's Church opposite the station at Feltham, Middlesex. Many tiles from the altar and nave were lifted with the consent of the vicar.

Relief-moulded majolica tile, Maw & Co., 6 x 4

JS2013.527.756

Maw & Co. majolica were just as good as Minton.

Encaustic tile, Minton & Co., 6 x 6

JS2013.527.768

Encaustic tiles, Minton & Co., 1865, 5 x 5

JS2013.527.771, JS2013.527.772, JS2013.527.769, JS2013.527.770

Right: Glazed encaustic tiles, Robert Minton Taylor, 6 x 6

JS2013.527.765, JS2013.527.767, JS2013.527.766

Swapped with Keith Horie for a spigot that had been in the back of my car for ages. The tile was meant to go on the gable end of his house, Fernbank.

Hand-painted tile, possibly by Morris & Co., 4 x 4

JS2013.527.776

The Lady of Shalott?

Glazed encaustic tiles, W. Godwin, c.1870, 4 x 4

JS2013.527.761, JS2013.527.762, JS2013.527.764, JS2013.527.763

Right: Encaustic tiles, Maw & Co., 6 x 6

JS2013.527.760, JS2013.527.759

Made for a conservatory. Very unusual secular design.

Encaustic tiles, Minton & Co., 1860, 6 x 6

JS2013.527.758, JS2013.527.757

Islamic-inspired border tiles.

Cuenca tile, Moorish design, Spain, date unknown, possibly 16th century, 3 x 3

JS2013.527.778

Encaustic tile, 3 x 3

JS2013.527.777

Encaustic tile, E. Smith & Co., Coalville, 6 x 6

JS2013.527.782

There is no entry in my magic records book of any purchase between 28 February and 9 April 2008. Even the items before and after these dates seem to have no relation to anything ceramic and indeed I have no memory at all of this tile. You might say why catalogue it? The truth is that it is different and quite stylish with strong Islamic affiliations. My wife will throw it out if it doesn't find a good home!

A very stylish and 'designed' tile with strong Japanese aspects. The florets in the corners call for a four-tile picture.

Sgraffito tile, Quentin Bell, 1970s, 5 x 5

JS2013.527.780

Very fine sgraffito work. Makes me dream of dear Edwin Martin, one of the four Martinware brothers, who specialised in sgraffito work.

Hand-painted tile from the 'Nursery Toys' series, designed by Dora Batty for Carter & Co., 1921–1923, 6 x 6

JS2013.527.779

Carter & Co. produced a huge range of hand-painted and stencilled tiles by many of the best artists in the field. Almost always very 'tiley'.

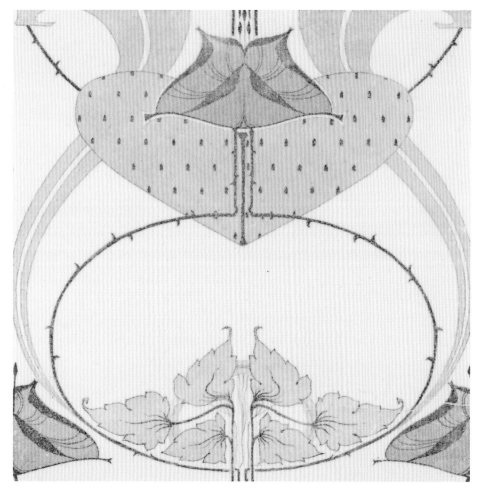

Left: Transfer-printed tile, designed by John Wadsworth, Minton China Works, c.1890, 6 x 6
JS2013.527.781

In my view the finest Art Nouveau English tile. By a miracle I bought nine at a Salvo Fair and framed together they make a fabulously complicated and satisfying design. Bless Anita Morgan for finding these. They had never been laid – probably a reserve pile in the event of emergency repairs. In my Top Five.

Transfer-printed tile, Sherwin and Cotton, 1881, 6 x 6
JS2013.527.783

Very aesthetic in style. Good for Oscar Wilde's patio.

Transfer-printed tile, Minton Hollins & Co., 6 x 6
JS2013.527.784

Transfer-printed c.1890 but could be 1960 – curious.

Encaustic tile, designed by A.W.N. Pugin, Minton & Co., c.1870, 6 x 6
JS2013.527.786

Extracted from the Birch Church, Manchester, I'm ninety percent certain that it was designed by A.W.N. Pugin.

Stencil decorated tile, possibly by a studio tile maker, H. & E. Smith blank, 1986, 6 x 6

JS2013.527.788

Can't find entry for this in my collecting journal. Very nice stylised image.

'Kookaburra', stencil decorated tile designed by Polly Brace for Dunsmore Tiles, Minton blank, 1928–1950, 6 x 6

JS2013.527.789

Block-printed tile, Minton Hollins & Co., 1868, 6 x 6

JS2013.527.785

Relief-moulded border tile, Craven Dunnill & Co., 6 x 6

JS2013.527.790

Surprisingly a few of these majolica are superbly executed; others are not so fine. My mind went to those cars with faults – made on Fridays at 4pm at the end of the week and lacking attention to detail.

Relief-moulded tile, Minton Hollins & Co., 6 x 6

JS2013.527.787

Put these round a dado rail and make a room palatial!

Relief-moulded majolica tile, Minton & Co.,
6 x 6

JS2013.527.792

Jewel-like in its sparkle. How splendiferous
to get three more to emphasise the border.
The most exquisite of English tiles. In my
Top Ten.

Relief-moulded tile, Craven Dunnill & Co., 6 x 6

JS2013.527.791

Jewel-like in design, colour and execution. An exquisite tile of great beauty. I do not believe any country produced tiles to equal these wonders of English mass production.

Relief-moulded majolica tile, Minton & Co., 6 x 6

JS2013.527.794

Strikingly novel and attractive.

Encaustic tile, W. Godwin, 6 x 6

JS2013.527.854

Above: Encaustic tiles, W. Godwin, 6 x 6

JS2013.527.855, JS2013.527.856, JS2013.527.857

Heraldic to create antique ambience with a glorious honey glaze and distressed finish.

Encaustic tile, W. Godwin, 4⅛ x 4⅛

JS2013.527.818

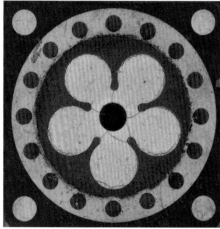

Encaustic tile, W. Godwin, 4⅛ x 4⅛

JS2013.527.853

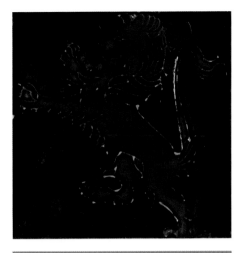

Tube-lined tile, Minton China Works, 6 x 6

JS2013.527.793

Encaustic tile, 4½ x 4½

JS2013.527.858

Relief-moulded tile, 4⅛ x 4⅛

JS2013.527.816

Encaustic tile, W. Godwin, 4⅛ x 4⅛

JS2013.527.817

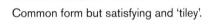

Encaustic tiles, W. Godwin, 5¾ x 5¾, 5⅞ x 5⅞

JS2013.527.814, JS2013.527.815

Common form but satisfying and 'tiley'.

Encaustic tile, Craven Dunnill & Co., 6 x 6

JS2013.527.810

Encaustic tile, Maw & Co., 6 x 6

JS2013.527.811

Attractive.

Encaustic tile, W. Godwin, 6 x 6

JS2013.527.812

Exquisite finish.

Encaustic tile, Minton & Co., 6 x 6

JS2013.527.813

Right: Encaustic tile, W. Godwin, 6 x 6

JS2013.527.808

A beautiful tile.

Encaustic tile, Minton & Co., 6 x 6

JS2013.527.806

What a charming figure. Why does nobody care for these little niceties today? This is why I collect beautiful odds and ends. What a joy to look at!

Encaustic tile, Minton & Co., 6 x 6

JS2013.527.807

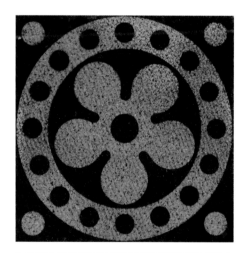

Encaustic tile, W. Godwin, 6 x 6

JS2013.527.804

Honey glaze and distressed.

Encaustic tile, W. Godwin, 6 x 6

JS2013.527.805

Encaustic tiles, Wedgwood, 2 x 2

JS2013.527.799, JS2013.527.800, JS2013.527.801,
JS2013.527.802

Encaustic tile, 6 x 6

JS2013.527.809

Interestingly quixotic.

Encaustic tile, W. Godwin, 4¼ x 4¼

JS2013.527.797

Encaustic tile, Craven Dunnill & Co.,
4¼ x 4¼

JS2013.527.795

Encaustic tile, Maw & Co., 4 x 4

JS2013.527.798

Encaustic tile, W. Godwin, 4¼ x 4¼

JS2013.527.796

Encaustic tile, W. Godwin, 4¼ x 4¼

JS2013.527.803

Encaustic tile, W. Godwin, 6 x 6

JS2013.527.832

The back has a more exciting mark than the front. A gift from Nicola Redway of Sotheby's.

Encaustic tile, Minton & Co., c.1840, 6 x 6

JS2013.527.833

These medieval-inspired tiles were first treated with yellow glaze to emulate the ancient form. This has been distressed by wear thus adding to its ancient aspect!

Relief-moulded tile, designed by C.F.A. Voysey as a self-portrait depicting the devil, J.C. Edwards (Ruabon), c.1900, 6 x 6

JS2013.527.834

Encaustic tile, designed by John Pollard Seddon, W. Godwin, 6 x 6

JS2013.527.828

Part of an ecclesiastical image which hopefully can be completed by the Ironbridge Gorge Museum and local supporters.

Encaustic tile, The Campbell Brick & Tile Co., 1875–1882, 6 x 6

JS2013.527.835

Such a powerful and striking design supposedly from Wemyss Castle. By a famous designer, but which?

Right: Encaustic tile, Minton & Co., 1871, 6 x 6

JS2013.527.829

A wonderfully strong and visually sustaining design of shape and colour. Only the hand of a master here! It would be nice to get three more.

Encaustic tile, designed for the Palace of Westminster, Minton & Co., 6 x 6

JS2013.527.830

A good example of a tile based on a medieval design.

Encaustic tile, Minton & Co., 6 x 6

JS2013.527.831

Glazed encaustic tile, 4½ x 4½

JS2013.527.821

Encaustic tile, designed by A.W.N. Pugin, Minton Hollins & Co., 6 x 6

JS2013.527.820

Five colour. Impeccable execution.

Left: Encaustic tiles, W. Godwin, 6 x 6

JS2013.527.824, JS2013.527.827, JS2013.527.825, JS2013.527.826

Encaustic tile, W. Godwin, 4 x 4

JS2013.527.823

A gorgeous design and impeccably made. No tile maker could surpass Godwin in encaustic quality.

Right: Encaustic tile, W. Godwin, 4½ x 4½

JS2013.527.822

Bought at the TACS jamboree at St Jude's Church Hall, Nottingham.

Printed tile, designed by A.W.N. Pugin, Robert Minton Taylor & Co., 1868, 8 x 8

JS2013.527.877

Design by A.W.N. Pugin, plate 30 in 'Floriated Ornament', 1849. Quite common. A lovely border that I have never seen in situ and more's the pity. Known in many varieties of colour. Printed but often hand-coloured to enrich and enliven the image.

Transfer-printed and hand-painted tile, Minton China Works, 7 x 7

JS2013.527.878

A riot of form and colour – lots of fun to amuse all ages! Frequently seen in different sizes and vast range of colourways. Would make a magnificent chair rail in a gracious mansion. Designed by Dresser.

Transfer-printed and hand-painted tile, Minton Hollins & Co., 9 x 9

JS2013.527.875

Very high quality design and execution – note the gold which adds lustre to the image. How much one would hope to make up a four- or sixteen-tile panel!

Transfer-printed and hand-painted tile, Minton Hollins & Co., 8 x 8

JS2013.527.876

Black field and two-tone green semi-formalized border. Very Dresser. The importance of having at least two repeats is immediately revealed when two border tiles are placed together. Overall it is a glorious design that is never a bore to behold.

Relief-moulded tile, Minton Hollins & Co., 8 x 8

JS2013.527.879

Interesting colourway of enthralling beauty. I'm inclined to think Owen Jones is the designer. Hopefully someone will find proof. I feel a great artist was responsible. Exquisite product, in my Top Five.

Transfer-printed tile, Minton & Co., c.1880, 8 x 8

JS2013.527.880

This was given to me by Dr Stuart Durant who is highly respected and well known as an expert on Christopher Dresser. It was designed by a famous man Ludwig Gruner, author of *Specimens of Oriental Art*, London, 1850. Delightfully quixotic in its kaleidoscope geometric pattern and colour. Never boring on the eye.

Hand-painted tile, Minton China Works,
8 x 8

JS2013.527.882

Exquisitely hand-painted tile so much in
the Japanese style that I believe it was
painted by a Japanese artist. I sold a similar
tile to British Museum signed in Japanese,
Shibiyami. In my Top Ten.

Border tile, Minton & Co., 8 x 8

JS2013.527.883

A rhapsody of geometry and wonder. One is never tired of gazing on this confection of black, gold and silver. 95% certain by Dresser. In my Top Ten.

Relief-moulded tile, Minton Hollins & Co., 8 x 8

JS2013.527.884

I am very impressed by this design and colour blend. Hopefully someone will find proof of the designer. I feel a good artist was responsible, perhaps Owen Jones or Christopher Dresser. In my Top Ten.

Block-printed and hand-painted tile, Minton China Works, 8 x 8

JS2013.527.887

Vast numbers of Victorian tiles were produced from different factories using anthemion designs of this form with widely different colourways, sizes and variations. I feel that this is so strong, confident and pleasing it must be 'designed' by one of the greats. Whether Owen Jones, Dresser or Seddon I hope further research will reveal.

Relief-moulded tile, Minton Hollins & Co., 8 x 8

JS2013.527.885

Very fine border.

Relief-moulded tile, Minton Hollins & Co., 8 x 8

JS2013.527.886

This needs further tiles to improve the effect.

Block-printed and hand-coloured tile, designed by A.W.N. Pugin, Minton & Co., 1895, 12 x 12

JS2013.527.898

So renowned and successful were Pugin's designs that they were used with some variations for many years after his death in 1851. Clive Wainwright was the chief mentor of all Gothic Revival collectors and fanatics. He pointed out the signs of an A.W.N. Pugin design. Notice the change in colour of leaves and foliage – such enhancement gives a three-dimensional effect to his floral designs. This tile well illustrates this feature.

Hand-painted aesthetic-style tile, Minton & Co., 6 x 6

JS2013.527.893

Hand-painted by Japanese artist. Bought with Seiz Saeki of Royal Doulton. He is Japanese, a very nice chap. The chipped corners indicate its use as part of appropriate Anglo-Japanese furniture. This was quite common when Japanese style was 'the' style. In my Top Twenty.

Encaustic tile, by Chris Cox of Craven Dunnill Jackfield Ltd, 2009, 12 x 12

JS2013.527.896

I had two made, one of which I gave to HRH Prince Charles. The other, this tile, was meant for the floor of a porch in Museum Street, Bloomsbury, as the original was worn out. However, the tenant was too busy fighting his landlord so never took up my offer of this tile.

Encaustic tile, Minton & Co., 12 x 12

JS2013.527.897

Coat of arms of Earl of Lovelace. A dear friend and I visited Portobello Market in c.1985 and I found one of these tiles for £50. I said you've got to buy that. But his wife, who is always anxious to avoid my supposed spendthrift influence on her husband, said no. He placated her by asserting he got it for £5! At the time of writing, this is worth £500–£1,000. These large heraldic tiles are very rare. I feel able to say this as I have been a collector for over 50 years; this experience gives a helpful perspective.

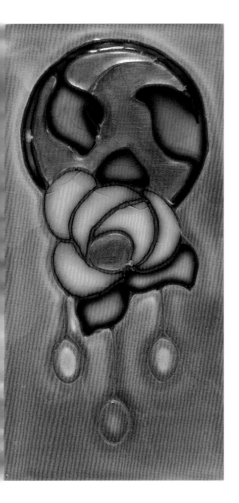

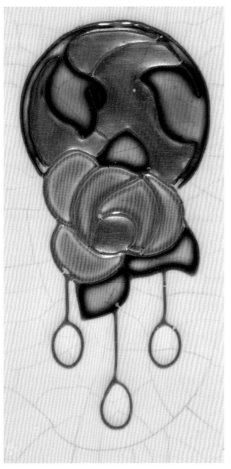

Transfer-printed tile, Minton & Co., c.1880, 8 x 8

JS2013.527.881

Left: Tube-lined Art Nouveau tiles, c.1910, 6 x 3

JS2013.527.894, JS2013.527.895

Very rich and beautiful finish. Bought from Adrian Grater, a gracious 'old world' Portobello dealer. One of the outstanding characters who greatly enriched the world of antiques. These two delectable jewels were once part of Gracie Fields's mansion in Bishops Avenue.

Block-printed and hand-coloured tile, possibly designed by Christopher Dresser, Minton Hollins & Co., 1872, 8 x 8

JS2013.527.888

Brilliantly vibrant and luxuriously exotic. A fantastic riot of colours. To behold a drawing room, its picture or dado rail enriched with such tiles, would be a sight beyond compare.

Block-printed and hand-painted tile, The Campbell Brick & Tile Co., 1875–1882, 8 x 8

JS2013.527.889

Perfect condition as if straight out of the showroom. A superb design, ideal for a conservatory or summer house.

Above: Block-printed tile, designed by Christopher Dresser, Minton & Co., 8 x 8

JS2013.527.890

Greek key-pattern tile, illustrated in Dresser's *Studies in Design*, bought in Art Deco Show in Town Hall, Kensington. This design is viewed with much more pleasure with a group of four or six tiles. It is so intricate that the eye is never bored by repetition. This is the vital characteristic of great design and is the ingredient that Dresser so skilfully achieves. I confess to extolling his merit – perhaps over much – but his mastery of tile design was often of the highest order.

Hand-painted stencilled tile, designed by Polly Brace for Dunsmore Tiles, c.1930, 8 x 8

JS2013.527.891

The Misses Brace and Fisher, 2 Hills Leigh Rd W8. Operating 1953–54. These two ladies were most inventive and devised a charming 'watery' glaze to make the images more realistic. They used blanks from other manufacturers.

Block-printed border tile, Minton Hollins & Co., 8 x 8

JS2013.527.892

I am almost certain that this was designed by Dresser – note his touch and style in the varied borders and the use of a black field to accentuate. An outstanding design greatly enhanced by the strong and exciting borders.

Encaustic tile, part of the Earl of Lovelace coat of arms, Minton & Co., 12 x 12

JS2013.527.899

This was made for Gothic additions to Guildford Lodge, East Horsley in Surrey. Memorial encaustics were often used in ecclesiastical buildings; they had the great merits of being very easy to clean and impervious to wear.

Block-printed tile, Minton Hollins & Co., 12 x 12

JS2013.527.900

This was bought with four other tiles from a fascinating small builder's yard which had an exciting pile of 4¼ encaustics.

Transfer-printed and hand-painted tile, Minton China Works, 12 x 12

JS2013.527.901

Lovely tile. Imagine a whole wall resplendent and enriched with candlelight. This is a later version of a Pugin design first used at the Palace of Westminster.

Encaustic tile, part of the Earl of Lovelace coat of arms, Minton & Co., 12 x 12

JS2013.527.902

All these tiles appeared at one time in 1975 at the much respected shop of Haslam & Whiteway. They were thought to be from the coat of arms of Earl of Lovelace and part of the additions to Guildford Lodge, East Horsley.

Hand-painted wax resist tile, Kenneth Clark Ceramics, 1970–1980s, 6 x 6

JS2013.527.935

Lovely strong tile in both design and colour. From Adrian Grater, Vernon Arcade, Portobello Road.

Designed by Lewis F. Day, Pilkington's Tile & Pottery Co. Ltd, 6 x 6

JS2013.527.931

One of Day's better designs.

Designed by Lewis F. Day, Pilkington's Tile & Pottery Co. Ltd, 6 x 6

JS2013.527.932

Designed by Lewis F. Day, Pilkington's Tile & Pottery Co. Ltd, 6 x 6

JS2013.527.933

Lewis F. Day lacks the vibrancy of William De Morgan in both design and colour.

Designed by Lewis F. Day, Pilkington's Tile & Pottery Co. Ltd, 6 x 6

JS2013.527.934

Designed by Lewis F. Day, 6 x 6

JS2013.527.936

Rather more adventurous for Lewis F. Day.

Designed by Lewis F. Day, 6 x 6

JS2013.527.937

Colossal variety in price but one must take an average – like stockbrokers!

Designed by Lewis F. Day, Pilkington's Tile & Pottery Co. Ltd, 6 x 6

JS2013.527.938

I call this disparagingly 'pretty, pretty'. On reflection perhaps I am too hard!

Block-printed and hand-painted tile, Minton & Co., 8 x 8

JS2013.527.944

Gorgeous.

Left: Majolica tile, Robert Minton Taylor & Co., c.1880, 8 x 8

JS2013.527.940

A masterpiece of design and execution, this is why we can claim this epoch as the greatest for Britain in the world of tile manufacture.

Relief-moulded tile, Minton Hollins & Co., 8 x 8

JS2013.527.941

Superb.

Relief-moulded tile, Minton Hollins & Co., 8 x 8

JS2013.527.942

A gift from Michael Whiteway for helping him to move his business from 20 Marloes Road, W8 to 105 Kensington Church Street. Gorgeous!

Relief-moulded Art Nouveau tile, Corn Brothers, 6 x 6

JS2013.527.939

An outstandingly strong Art Nouveau tile, probably bought in Portobello in the late 1960s.

Block-printed tile, Minton China Works, 8 x 8

JS2013.527.945

Really a wallpaper design.

Encaustic tile, Minton & Co., 1862, 4½ diameter

JS2013.527.929

Probably an A.W.N. Pugin design.

Sgraffito tile, Quentin Bell, 1970s, 4 x 4

JS2013.527.927

Bought at an exhibition by Andy Tilbrook. A charming, different and modern approach.

Lustre tile, designed by Jonathan Chiswell Jones, 2008, 6 x 6

JS2013.527.930

Contemporary artist at his Christmas present Exhibition. He is magnificent. His finish is so lustrous.

Transfer-printed tile, Minton China Works, 8 x 8

JS2013.527.943

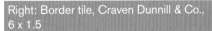

Right: Border tile, Craven Dunnill & Co., 6 x 1.5

JS2013.527.928

I did not intend to catalogue these strip border tiles. But they do proclaim the pains that the early manufacturers took to produce such charming and beautiful effects.

Encaustic tile, Minton Hollins & Co., 1846, 4 x 4

JS2013.527.955

Encaustic tiles, W. Godwin, 4 x 4

JS2013.527.947, JS2013.527.946, JS2013.527.948, JS2013.527.949

A glorious ensemble of Godwin encaustics of great strength and character. Saved from Holy Trinity Church, Wimbledon.

Encaustic tiles, Minton Hollins & Co., 4 x 4

JS2013.527.950, JS2013.527.951, JS2013.527.953, JS2013.527.952

JS2013.527.954

Secular encaustic. A very beautiful set of tiles – much improved by display as a set of nine.

Encaustic tile, W. Godwin, 6 x 6

JS2013.527.956

One of 25 encaustics bought from Neil Phillips. They needed a lot of cement removed with Wolf angle grinder.

Encaustic border tile, W. Godwin, 6 x 6

JS2013.527.957

Encaustic tile, Minton & Co., 1871, 6 x 6

JS2013.527.959

I imagine this kaleidoscope being made up, in my dreams, by the tile designer. He is lost for a suitable new Gothic design. No worries – insert a pile of polychrome trefoils, quatrefoils, multi-foils, squares, triangles etc and shake them all about. Apply eye to the viewer. The result is constant variety.

Encaustic tile, Minton & Co., 6 x 6

JS2013.527.958

I shall probably never find the other 15 tiles to complete the picture. It is utterly infuriating and frustrating that they were left behind. This reminds me of the man who had six children. Anticipating arguments over his will he left two exquisite matching chairs, from a set of 12, to each one. The total is worth vastly more than the parts. So, much of my time is spent searching for tiles to make up sets!

Encaustic tile, Minton & Co., 6 x 6

JS2013.527.960

Highly likely to be designed by A.W.N. Pugin. Oh, so satisfying on the eye! Restful in any church building. Note the playful 'kick backs' to dispel boredom.

Encaustic tile, W. Godwin, 6 x 6

JS2013.527.961

This one is Godwin; most of the tiles from his factory in Lugwardine were glazed and of unsurpassed quality of colour, tonality and sheer finish. Compare with the crude continental Villeroy & Boch. These superb products justify my assertion of the pre-eminence of English tiles in this epoch.

Encaustic tile, Chris Cox, Craven Dunnill Jackfield Ltd, 2009, 8 x 9

JS2013.527.963

A gift from Chris Cox, the expert encaustic tile maker of Craven Dunnill Jackfield Ltd. A fine product, that is just as good, if not better than its 19th-century counterparts. We should all try to expand this business. All those Victorian palaces in India and civic buildings in New Zealand and Australia will need new encaustic floors sometime soon!

Encaustic tile, W. Godwin, 6 x 6

JS2013.527.962

A pleasing variation of colourways.

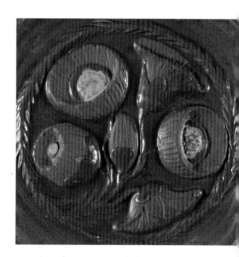

Relief-moulded tile, Maw & Co., 4 x 4

JS2013.527.965

Screen-printed tile, designed by Leslie Elsden, Carter & Co., 1960s, 4 x 4

JS2013.527.964

So much of my life has been taken up with my property company and my work on trying to improve the built environment (through the Pembridge Association and the Notting Hill Gate Improvements Group) that I have not researched my tile collection as I should. I am hoping Chris Blanchett and TACS will fill in the huge gaps. I love Carter as they always have good artists.

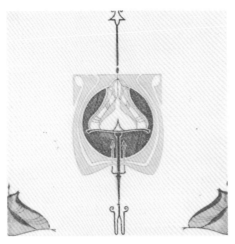

Art Nouveau tile, designed by John Wadsworth, Minton & Co., 6 x 6

JS2013.527.966

In my view the finest Art Nouveau tile designer. This tile desperately needs at least nine more to make a decent repeat. Can you please find some for us?

Block-printed border tile, Minton & Co., 8 x 8

JS2013.527.967

Right: Relief-moulded tile, Craven Dunnill & Co., 5 x 4

JS2013.527.968

I suspect this may be an Owen Jones design inspired by his studies of the Alhambra in Granada, Spain. This tile perfectly exemplifies my 'tile dreams' of finding more to complete an adequate run. What a glorious picture they would make!

Transfer-printed tile from the 'Farm' series, designed by William Wise, Minton China Works, 6 x 6

JS2013.527.969

An ideal tile for a farm shop.

Relief-moulded tile, The Campbell Brick & Tile Co., 6 x 6

JS2013.527.973

As I have a Japanese wife, Takko, I am interested in all things Japanese. In 1959 I organised an Oxford and Cambridge University rugby tour of Japan. That was my first visit and we have often returned to visit Takko's parents and extended family. Enormous interest in Japan spread extensively in England from the latter part of the 19th century. Christopher Dresser made a long visit to Japan and published *Japan: Its Architecture, Art & Art Manufactures* in 1882. This is superbly instructive and fascinating. Dresser's knowledge and huge interest in all things Japanese has enriched his multitudinous influence on decorative art. Maybe he designed this tile.

Relief-moulded majolica tile, early Minton & Co., c.1840, 4 x 4

JS2013.527.971

An excellent blend of English and Islamic styles.

Block-printed tile, designed by Christopher Dresser, Minton & Co., c.1875, 6 x 6

JS2013.527.970

Probably Dr Dresser's most famous and early design, much copied in varied fields and formats. A delightful mélange of Anglo-Japanese art.

Opposite: Silk-screen printed tiles from the 'Pub Game' series, designed by Reginald Till, Carter & Co., early 1950s, 6 x 6

JS2013.527.975, JS2013.527.972

Very collectable.

Transfer-printed tile, 6 x 6

JS2013.527.974

I find this tile the very epitome of the aesthetic, very pleasing to my eye with a stylised rising and setting sun. If this is not by Dresser it was designed by someone with an excellent 'touch'.

Transfer-printed tile, 6 x 6

JS2013.527.976

Transfer-printed tile, 6 x 6

JS2013.527.977

Block-printed tiles, designed by Lewis F. Day, Minton & Co., c.1880, 6 x 6

JS2013.527.978, JS2013.527.981, JS2013.527.980

Very rich in form and colour although on the whole I consider him a weak designer when compared with Dresser, Voysey, William De Morgan et al.

Relief-moulded tile, Godwin and Hewitt, 6 x 6

JS2013.527.979

Particularly enchanting and rare – hops, birds and flying insect. Bought from Peter Goddard – far too expensive but I feel it wise to encourage him in the hope of future pearls! He drives over to show me his finds of an evening so I don't feel I should haggle too much.

Encaustic tile, Minton & Co., 6 x 6

JS2013.527.983

As soon as doves appear on a tile, enthusiastic vendors quickly rush to attribute it to Voysey and adjust the price accordingly! In truth I believe it is more a Christian symbol – the doves of peace …

Relief-moulded tile, Minton & Co., 6 x 6

JS2013.527.982

An excellent very strong design in the Gothic style with Christian symbols.

Medieval design, encaustic tile panel, W. Godwin, 9 x 9

JS2013.527.984

Left: Encaustic tiles, Minton & Co., 6 x 6

JS2013.527.989, JS2013.527.986, JS2013.527.987, JS2013.527.988

A very fine design.

Right: Encaustic tiles, designed by A.W.N. Pugin, Minton & Co., 6 x 6

JS2013.527.991, JS2013.527.993, JS2013.527.990, JS2013.527.994, JS2013.527.992

From the Birch Church, Manchester.

Left: Encaustic tiles, Minton & Co., 1880, 6 x 6

JS2013.527.997, JS2013.527.995, JS2013.527.998, JS2013.527.996

A very lively design that is fascinatingly quixotic and unusually secular.

Transfer-printed tile, Minton Hollins & Co., 1878, 6 x 6

JS2013.527.999

Smacks of Christopher Dresser, highly inventive design, never boring.

Encaustic tile, Minton & Co., 5¾ x 5¾

JS2013.527.1000

Encaustic tile, Minton Hollins & Co., 3 x 3

JS2013.527.1001

Encaustic tile, Maw & Co., 3 x 3

JS2013.527.1002

Encaustic tile, W. Godwin, 4 x 4

JS2013.527.1003

Encaustic tile, Craven Dunnill & Co., 4 x 4

JS2013.527.1004

Encaustic tile, Robert Minton Taylor & Co., 1871–1874, 6½ x 6½

JS2013.527.985

Left: Encaustic tiles, Minton & Co., 1857, 6 x 6

JS2013.527.1110, JS2013.527.1111, JS2013.527.1009, JS2013.527.1112

Very striking. The anthemion strikes again!

Encaustic tiles, Minton & Co., 6 x 6

**JS2013.527.1008, JS2013.527.1007, JS2013.527.1006,
JS2013.527.1005**

I was very thrilled at finding this as it has
eight colours.

Encaustic tiles, Maw & Co., 6 x 4

JS2013.527.1113, JS2013.527.1114

Outstanding. Eight colour, in my Top Twenty, a masterpiece of the encaustic art.

Encaustic tiles, Maw & Co., 6 x 6

JS2013.527.1115, JS2013.527.1181

Crystal Tea Urn Stand, 10 x 10

JS2013.527.1116

Printed mosaic-style tile, Copeland, 10½ x 10½

JS2013.527.1117

Tea pot stand. Probably inspired by excavations at Pompeii or London.

Block-printed and hand-painted tile, designed by A.W.N. Pugin, Minton & Co., 10½ x 10½

JS2013.527.1119

Block-printed and hand-coloured tile, designed by A.W.N. Pugin, Minton & Co., 8½ x 8½

JS2013.527.1120

Block-printed and hand-painted tile, designed by A.W.N. Pugin, Minton & Co., c.1855, 12 x 12

JS2013.527.1118

Bought at Jeremy Cooper's Christmas tile sale. A glistening extravaganza in silver and gold.

Encaustic tile, W. Godwin, 9 diameter

JS2013.527.1121

The oak frame was a collection bowl from a demolished church.

Transfer-printed tile, designed by John Moyr Smith, Minton & Co., c.1880, 7½ x 7½ in frame

JS2013.527.1122

Moyr Smith was part of Christopher Dresser's studio. An extensive controversy exists as to which designs were by Dresser and which by John Moyr Smith.

Tile designed by Martin Brothers, 1897, 8 x 8

JS2013.527.1123

Typical extensive, dark brown foliage with magical dragon hidden in the forestry.

Encaustic tile, W. Godwin, 4¼ x 4¼

JS2013.527.1126

A magnificent little tile and I much look forward to knowing the name of the designer.

Encaustic tile, W. Godwin, 4¼ x 4¼

JS2013.527.1130

A majestic tile and rightful to honour to a dearly departed friend.

Relief-moulded majolica tile, Maw & Co.,
4 x 6

JS2013.527.1303

Very attractive majolica.

Right: Encaustic tiles, W. Godwin, 6 x 6

JS2013.527.1298, JS2013.527.1297

Part of a typical John Pollard Seddon
design, from Sunningwell Church,
Oxfordshire. Acquired in a swap with Bob
Smith. He was a true tile lover combined
with a love of cars – the tiles were laid flat
on sand in his garage and with care the car
was parked on top of the lot.

Left: Relief-moulded encaustic tiles,
Craven Dunnill & Co., 6 x 6

JS2013.527.1302, JS2013.527.1301, JS2013.527.1300

Waiting for the fourth!

Encaustic tile, Minton & Co., 5¾ x 5¾

JS2013.527.1299

Encaustic tiles, J.C. Edwards (Ruabon),
4¼ x 4¼

**JS2013.527.1304, JS2013.527.1307, JS2013.527.1305,
JS2013.527.1306**

Right: Encaustic tiles, The Campbell Brick
& Tile Co., 4¼ x 4¼

**JS2013.527.1310, JS2013.527.1309, JS2013.527.1308,
JS2013.527.1311**

A very beautiful configuration. The design
and colourways sit superbly on the 4 tiles.

Encaustic tile, designed by A.W.N. Pugin, Minton & Co., 6 x 6

JS2013.527.1313

This is probably the most common floor tile design by A.W.N. Pugin and was used extensively in George Edmund Street's Royal Courts of Justice.

Encaustic tiles, W. Godwin, 6 x 6

JS2013.527.1317, JS2013.527.1315, JS2013.527.1316, JS2013.527.1314

From Loughton Parish Church, Hereford.

Left: Encaustic tiles, Minton & Co., 1864, 6 x 6

JS2013.527.1320, JS2013.527.1319, JS2013.527.1318, JS2013.527.1321

Very common design. These were salvaged from 16–34 Blenheim Crescent, Notting Hill Housing Trust.

Left: Glazed encaustic tiles, The Campbell Brick & Tile Co., 6 x 6

JS2013.527.1372, JS2013.527.1370, JS2013.527.1371, JS2013.527.1369

Right: Glazed encaustic tiles, W. Godwin, 6 x 6

JS2013.527.1323, JS2013.527.1322, JS2013.527.1325, JS2013.527.1324

The impression is given of a Ducal Crown indecipherable with antiquity.

Left: Glazed encaustic tiles, W. Godwin, 6 x 6

JS2013.527.1327, JS2013.527.1326, JS2013.527.1329, JS2013.527.1328

Right: Glazed encaustic tiles, Minton & Co., 6 x 6

JS2013.527.1330, JS2013.527.1331, JS2013.527.1332, JS2013.527.1333

This is a most common encaustic Minton design and I have seen at least ten varieties of colourway. This is a particularly bright and lively version.

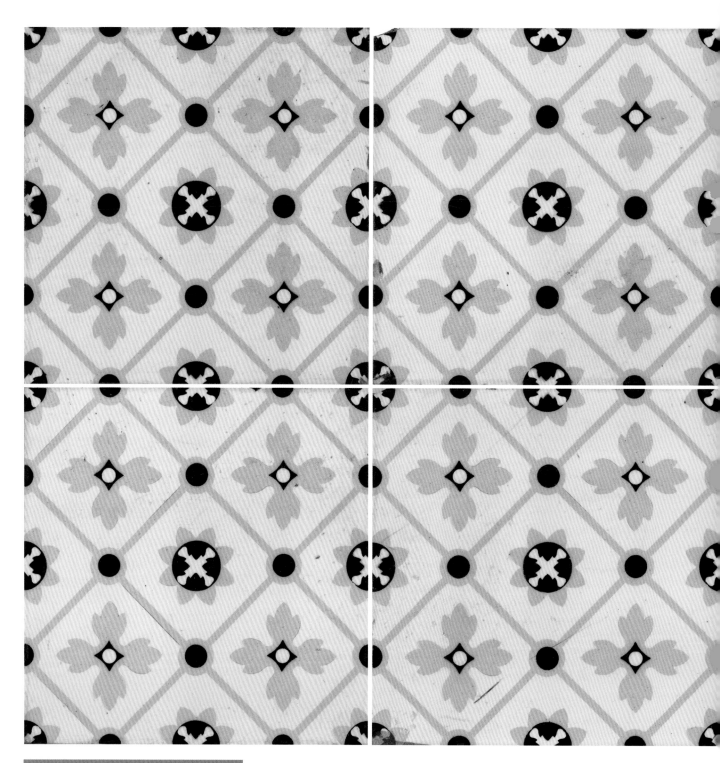

Glazed encaustic tiles, W. Godwin, 6 x 6

JS2013.527.1334, JS2013.527.1337, JS2013.527.1335,
JS2013.527.1336

The black and gold inlay on a white field
make for an unusual mélange.

Block-printed and hand-painted tiles, designed by Christopher Dresser, Minton Hollins & Co., 6 x 6

JS2013.527.1354, JS2013.527.1355, JS2013.527.1358

From 1850–1904 Dresser was the greatest and most popular designer in Europe and in my view vastly superior to William Morris. I have seen this design in many sizes and colourways – probably over fifty. It is very satisfying. Note the great care and panache applied by him to the top and bottom borders – so carefully conceived but different.

Block-printed tiles, Maw & Co., c.1860, 6 x 6

JS2013.527.1357, JS2013.527.1356, JS2013.527.1359, JS2013.527.1360

I greatly enjoy these anthemion border tiles. Note how important it is to reveal the whole pattern.

Below: Encaustic tiles, The Campbell Brick & Tile Co., 6 x 6

JS2013.527.1351, JS2013.527.1352, JS2013.527.1350, JS2013.527.1345, JS2013.527.1346, JS2013.527.1343, JS2013.527.1353, JS2013.527.1349, JS2013.527.1342, JS2013.527.1347, JS2013.527.1344, JS2013.527.1340, JS2013.527.1348, JS2013.527.1341, JS2013.527.1338, JS2013.527.1339

Altar step for those kneeling prior to partaking of bread and wine.

JS2013.527.1362, JS2013.527.1361

More anthemions. A very strong design motif.

Encaustic tiles, Minton & Co., 1850, 6 x 6

JS2013.527.1364, JS2013.527.1363, JS2013.527.1365

Right: Transfer-printed border tile, 5¾ x 2¾

JS2013.527.1367

The stylised anthemion is used more than any other flower (in various forms, some more charming and successful than others) in Victorian design. This is particularly so in tiles. I am sure this design is from a master. Dresser springs to mind, but it is irritating that most dealers throw in his name to enhance the price! In my Top Twenty.

Glazed encaustic tiles, W. Godwin, 4 x 4

JS2013.527.1374, JS2013.527.1377, JS2013.527.1378,
JS2013.527.1375, JS2013.527.1388, JS2013.527.1385,
JS2013.527.1386, JS2013.527.1387, JS2013.527.1376

I greatly love these small Godwin encaustics. The picture is best probably with 16 tiles! Four are needed, nine would be better but a panel of a hundred or so would be spectacular. In my Top Twenty.

Right: Encaustic border tile, c.1875, 5¾ x 2¾

JS2013.527.1366

Crowns were popular and it did not mean that the owner was a duke or an earl.

Block-printed tile, Minton China Works, 6 x 6

JS2013.527.1368

Encaustic tile, Minton & Co., 6¾ x 6¾

JS2013.527.1373

Glazed encaustic tile, Craven Dunnill & Co., 4 x 4

JS2013.527.1383

Right: Glazed encaustic tile, Maw & Co., 6 x 4

JS2013.527.1379

Glazed encaustic tile, W. Godwin, 4 x 4

JS2013.527.1384

Glazed encaustic tile, Minton & Co., 6 x 3

JS2013.527.1380

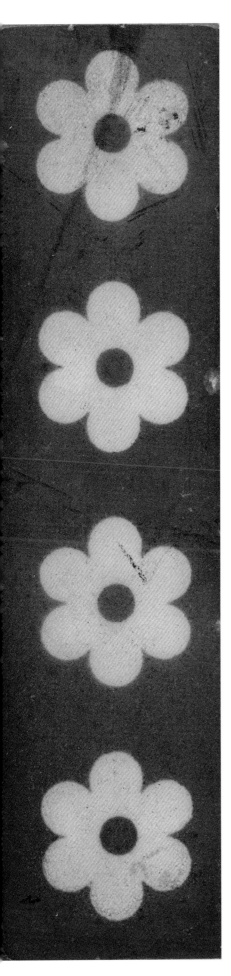

Encaustic tile, designed by John Pollard Seddon, Maw & Co., 5 x 5

JS2013.527.1389

Encaustic tile, Minton & Co., 4½ x 4½

JS2013.527.1390

Encaustic tiles, Minton & Co., 6 x 6

JS2013.527.1403, JS2013.527.1401,
JS2013.527.1402, JS2013.527.1404

Encaustic tile, 6 x 1½

JS2013.527.1381

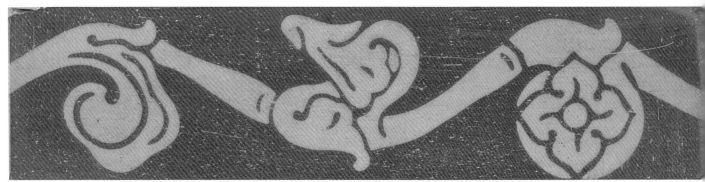

Encaustic tile, Craven Dunnill & Co., 6 x 1½

JS2013.527.1382

Opposite: Relief-moulded majolica tiles, designed by Christopher Dresser, Maw & Co., 6 x 6

JS2013.527.1393, JS2013.527.1394, JS2013.527.1392, JS2013.527.1391

Heavy Egyptian inspiration, designed by Dr Dresser. Well-known exhibition piece.

Right: Encaustic tiles, Maw & Co., 4 x 4

JS2013.527.1398, JS2013.527.1397, JS2013.527.1400, JS2013.527.1399

Glazed encaustic tiles, Minton & Co., 1867, 6 x 6

JS2013.527.1395, JS2013.527.1396, JS2013.527.1405, JS2013.527.1406

Strong design.

Encaustic border tile, Hargreaves & Craven, Jackfield, 3 x 6

JS2013.527.1415

Right: Encaustic tiles, St George's Tile Works, 6 x 6

JS2013.527.1409, JS2013.527.1410, JS2013.527.1408, JS2013.527.1407

Lovely, lovely glaze. Bought from Haslam and Whiteway.

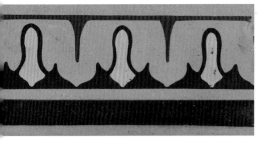

Encaustic tile, Minton & Co., 3 x 6

JS2013.527.1416

Marvellous.

Right: Glazed encaustic tiles, Minton & Co., 6 x 6

JS2013.527.1411, JS2013.527.1412, JS2013.527.1414, JS2013.527.1413

Very exciting dramatic white field by … someone!

Glazed encaustic tile, Malkin Edge & Co., c.1900, 7 x 7

JS2013.527.1418

The pattern in just one tile permits the eye a feast of squares and quatrefoils; if there were four tiles the pattern would be further enriched.

Encaustic tile, Maw & Co., 7 x 7

JS2013.527.1417

Just an attractive pattern enriched by having four tiles which open up a series of patterns. The eye is thus very unlikely to be bored.

Left: Encaustic tiles, Minton & Co., c.1895, 6 x 6

JS2013.527.1421, JS2013.527.1425, JS2013.527.1422, JS2013.527.1420, JS2013.527.1424, JS2013.527.1423, JS2013.527.1426, JS2013.527.1427

Compelling! Four more needed.

Encaustic tile, possibly designed by A.W.N. Pugin, Minton & Co., 6 x 6

JS2013.527.1419

This is quite probably an A.W.N. Pugin design. He exhorted Sir Herbert Minton to enrich the existing red and buff encaustic tiles with blue. This range was later extended to other colours. Pugin and Minton enjoyed an immensely strong understanding; all those who see their work are beneficiaries of their genius.

Encaustic tiles, W. Godwin, 6 x 6

JS2013.527.1429, JS2013.527.1431, JS2013.527.1430, JS2013.527.1428

Glazed encaustic tiles, Minton & Co., 6 x 6

JS2013.527.1433, JS2013.527.1434, JS2013.527.1435, JS2013.527.1432

Gorgeous for a conservatory or even a greenhouse.

Glazed encaustic tiles, possibly designed by A.W.N. Pugin, Minton & Co., c.1840, 6 x 6

JS2013.527.1436, JS2013.527.1439, JS2013.527.1437, JS2013.527.1438

Slightly distressed surface – heavily inspired by the medieval.

Glazed encaustic tiles, Minton & Co., 6 x 6

JS2013.527.1441, JS2013.527.1442, JS2013.527.1443, JS2013.527.1440

A joy to the eye.

Glazed encaustic tiles, Chamberlain & Co., 1840–1848, 6 x 6

JS2013.527.1444, JS2013.527.1445, JS2013.527.1446

This company made tiles of great beauty, mostly encaustics inspired by medieval patterns. The honeyed glaze and very subtle distressing first noted by Kenneth Beaulah make this factory pre-eminent in the field of 'antique-looking' encaustics.

Encaustic tile, W. Godwin, 4¼ x 4¼

JS2013.527.1447

The quality of manufacture, the precision of the painters and the brilliance of the glazing make these into objets d'art to me. I cherish them. They make marvellous coasters for glasses of wine on a smart Gallé marquetry table. In my Top Twenty.

Glazed encaustic tile, Minton & Co., c.1880, 4½ x 4½

JS2013.527.1448

Unusual black field is enriching.

Encaustic tile, W. Godwin, 6 x 6

JS2013.527.1449

Encaustic tile, W. Godwin, 6 x 6

JS2013.527.1450

Cinquefoil symbolizes the five wounds of Jesus Christ.

Encaustic tile, W. Godwin, 6 x 6

JS2013.527.1451

Glazed encaustic tile, Minton & Co., 6 x 6

JS2013.527.1452

I love this tile – strongly inspired by the
Egyptian style, with a lovely black field
and bright red stylised flowers. Very much
Dresser's hand! I paid a ridiculous price, but
this happens at auctions. You have to bid to
get it and you have to have the cash too! I
only got one, four or eight would be lovely,
sixteen paradise! A room on its own. Just
candlelight.

Encaustic tile, Minton & Co., 6 x 6

JS2013.527.1453

Encaustic tile, W. Godwin, 6 x 6

JS2013.527.1454

Encaustic tile, Minton & Co., c.1860, 6 x 6

JS2013.527.1455

Encaustic tile, W. Godwin, 6 x 6

JS2013.527.1456

I find this increasingly attractive and an extraordinary reproduction of the 15th-century original.

Encaustic tile, Minton & Co., c.1840, 6 x 6

JS2013.527.1457

Probably inspired by medieval tiles, with a rich honey glaze.

Encaustic tile, Minton & Co., c.1840, 6 x 6

JS2013.527.1458

This design is copied from tiles in Westminster Abbey.

Encaustic tile, W. Godwin, 6 x 6

JS2013.527.1460

Encaustic tile, designed by A.W.N. Pugin for the Palace of Westminster, Minton & Co., c.1850, 6 x 6

JS2013.527.1461

In my Top Twenty.

Glazed encaustic tile, W. Godwin, 4 x 4

JS2013.527.1462

Brilliant in design and execution.

Left: Glazed encaustic tile, Minton & Co., 6 x 6

JS2013.527.1459

A forcefully strong image.

Encaustic tile, Minton & Co., 1858, 4 x 4

JS2013.527.1463

'God not fortune' … a laudable family motto, but which family?

Encaustic tile, Maw & Co., 4½ x 4½

JS2013.527.1465

Glazed encaustic tile, Minton Hollins & Co., 4½ x 4½

JS2013.527.1464

Not a 'tiley' design, more apt for a lady's bonnet or wallpaper, but very rare and a beautiful eight-colour encaustic. In my Top Five.

Glazed encaustic tile, Minton Hollins & Co., 1868, 4 x 4

JS2013.527.1466

A fabulous design, ideally used in a panel of 9, 16 or 25.

Glazed encaustic tile, W. Godwin, 4 x 4

JS2013.527.1467

Right: Hand-painted tile panel, William De Morgan, 1888–1897, 16¼ x 32½

JS2013.527.1741

I do think a glamorous tile picture is immeasurably enriched by border tiles and an oak frame. Delectable! The Prince of English tile makers.

Encaustic tile panel, W. Godwin, 17 x 17

JS2013.527.1758

Note that many of these Godwin tiles have a most interesting 'distressed' surface. This manufacturer's trick was much practised by Godwin of Lugwardine, and much enhanced the antique effect. This was first noted by dear Kenneth Beaulah of TACS. Lovely. In my Top 100.

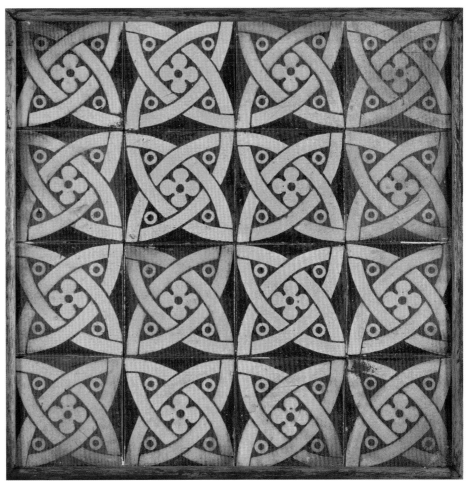

Encaustic tile panel, Craven Dunnill & Co., 18 x 18

JS2013.527.1757

See how much better they look in such a mass than just one, or even four.

Left: Encaustic tile panel, Minton & Co., c.1860, 19 x 19

JS2013.527.1506

This came from the Birch Church in Manchester. I bought all the tiles as the church was being converted into a residence as I recollect.

Right: Encaustic tile, Minton & Co., 1867, 12½ x 12½

JS2013.527.1598

Encaustic tile depicting Medusa, Minton & Co., 1895, 15 diameter

JS2013.527.1595

This was the centrepiece of a large floor ordered by the American millionaire, Mr Astor, for his residence at Cliveden, Buckinghamshire. My most lucky find. Not quite Tutankhamun's death mask but still … Bought from dealer in Jones Arcade and previously owned by the daughter of the surveyor supervising the improvements at Cliveden in 1904. The head of Medusa is the centrepiece, a full description of which is set out in the *Pottery Gazette* of 1 November 1895. The destruction of this floor tops the list of awful losses of much of Britain's cultural heritage. I weep. (see p.354)

JS2013.527.1570

These designs draw heavily on the medieval I shall refrain from using the word 'copy' but there is often no significant difference. The excellent medieval examples in the British Museum will be a valuable comparison.

JS2013.527.1671

This was also part of the great Cliveden House mosaic pavement, which measured thirty by forty feet. Nancy Astor ordered the removal of the fabulous pavement in 1904 and part of it now lies in the basement of Cliveden.

JS2013.527.1569

Most people would be happy with four but 16 make a better image.

Encaustic tile panel, St George's Tile
Works, 12½ x 18½

JS2013.527.1681

n ancient times fragments of stained glass
were stuck together so I feel at liberty
to do the same with tiles. Very beautiful,
distressed surface encaustics.

Encaustic tile panel, copy of a medieval design from Penn in Buckinghamshire, Architectural Pottery Co., 12½ x 18½

JS2013.527.1673

Relief-moulded tile panel, The Campbell Brick & Tile Co., 19½ x 13½

JS2013.527.1680

Fine border tiles of great effect.

Encaustic tile panel, St George's Tile Works, 12½ x 18½

JS2013.527.1681

Relief-moulded majolica tile panel, designed by Christopher Dresser for the Paris International Exhibition, Maw & Co., 1867, 35 x 22½

JS2013.527.1588

Great. In my Top 100.

JS2013.527.1584

This picture was made for a W.H. Smith shop. Eric
Gill designed the lettering but it is under investigation
by a researcher at the Museum of London as to who
designed the rest of the panel.

Right: Encaustic tile panel, W. Godwin,
18 x 18

JS2013.527.1551

Godwin tiles were very popular with the
'nouveau riche', anxious that their Gothic pile
should indicate a long ancestral heritage!

Encaustic tile panel, Minton & Co., 19 x 19

JS2013.527.1500

Remember Pugin dedicated his work to
the glory of God and his churches were
to be magnificent offerings of thanks to
the majesty of the Almighty. The constant
interplay of trefoil and quatrefoil are intended
to remind us of holy symbols.

HALLWAYS

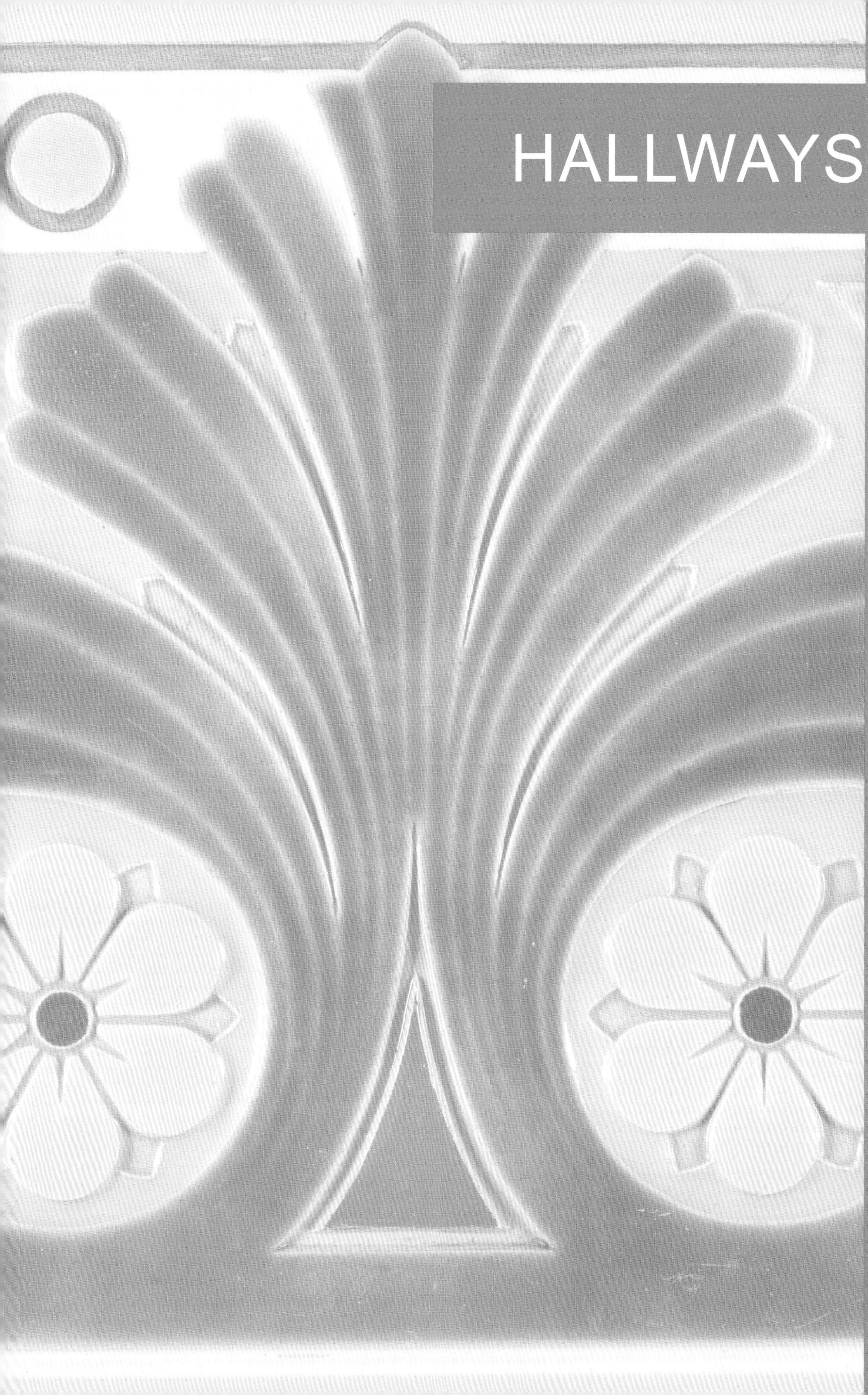

Encaustic tile panel, showing the Blackmore family coat of arms, Minton & Co., 1866, 16 x 16

JS2013.527.1508

In my Top Fifty, lovely.

Encaustic tile panel, featuring the monogram of William Blackmore, Minton & Co., 1886, 19 x 19

JS2013.527.1593

Encaustic border tile, The Campbell Brick & Tile Co., c.1875, 6 x 3

JS2013.527.27

Lovely Dresseresque border tile.

Encaustic border tile, Minton & Co., 5⅝ x 3⅛

JS2013.527.28

Encaustic tile, Minton & Co., 4 x 4

JS2013.527.24

Muddled reference in catalogue but must record that I bought these from Bernadette Heatherington, a very successful dealer in 19th- and 20th-century decorative art. I was a rugby friend of her husband.

Encaustic tile panel, T.W. Walker, c.1860, 12½ x 12½

JS2013.527.1759

Right: Encaustic tile, Westminster Abbey Chapter House, Minton & Co., c.1840, 6 x 1½

JS2013.527.25

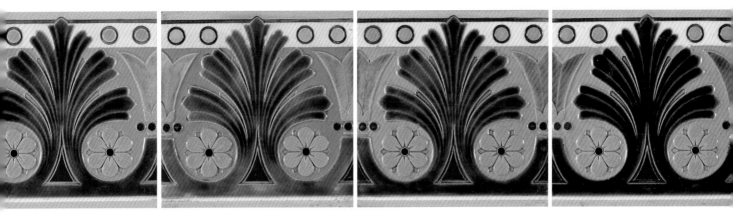

Relief-moulded majolica tiles, Minton Hollins & Co., 7¾ x 7¾

JS2013.527.1273, JS2013.527.1272, JS2013.527.1275, JS2013.527.1274

Superb design that is in my Top Ten.

Encaustic border tile, Minton & Co., 5⅞ x 3

JS2013.527.30

Relief-moulded tile, Maw & Co., 5⅝ x 3

JS2013.527.31

Encaustic border tile, 5¾ x 1¾

JS2013.527.26

Glazed encaustic tile, Minton & Co.,
4¼ x 4¼

JS2013.527.29

Encaustic tile, Minton & Co., 1861, 6 x 6

JS2013.527.33

Encaustic border tile, Maw & Co., c.1880,
6 x 4

JS2013.527.32

Very striking border tile. What a huge
amount of careful work for just a border tile,
but what a brilliant effect!

Encaustic tile, monogram for John Talbot,
Earl of Shrewsbury, designed by A.W.N.
Pugin, Minton & Co., 1860, 6 x 6

JS2013.527.34

From St Mary's Convent, Birmingham.

Transfer-printed tile depicting biblical
scene, original design by John Moyr Smith,
Minton China Works, 6 x 6

JS2013.527.42

Moyr Smith whose design of furniture,
clothing, vases, headgear and everything
you could think of is very much in the
'Dresser' style. Moyr Smith clearly learned a
lot from his time at the Dresser studio!

Encaustic tile, Minton & Co., 1871, 6 x 6

JS2013.527.44

THE JOHN SCOTT TILE COLLECTION

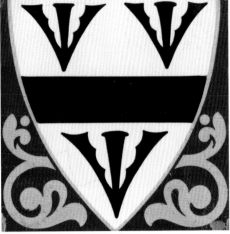

Encaustic tiles depicting heraldic shields, Minton & Co., 5 x 5

JS2013.527.35, JS2013.527.36

Fanciful crests were quite common as colourful displays of nobility or aspirations to nobility.

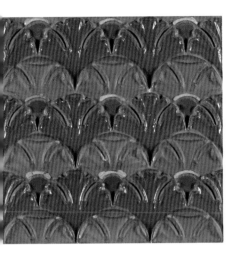

Relief-moulded tile, Maw & Co., 6 x 6

JS2013.527.38

Very beautiful in relief.

Block-printed tile, designed by A.W.N. Pugin, Minton China Works, c.1880, 8 x 8

JS2013.527.43

Probably derived from historical forms.

Block-printed and hand-coloured tile, designed by A.W.N. Pugin, Minton China Works, 1868–1900, 6 x 6

JS2013.527.45

Encaustic tile depicting a dove of peace, Minton & Co., 6 x 6

JS2013.527.46

Bought in excellent condition at the Kensington Town Hall Fair.

Encaustic tile, designed by A.W.N. Pugin, Minton & Co., 6 x 6

JS2013.527.39

Used by G.E. Street in the Law Courts on the Strand. Possibly the most common Victorian encaustic tile of them all.

Relief-moulded portrait of Evelyn Shepard aged three, modelled from a photograph possibly by Hedley Tilsed for Carter & Co., c.1910, 6 x 6

JS2013.527.47

No, this is not the young Napoleon! A boy of one of the Carter & Co. staff.

Relief-moulded tile depicting the coat of arms of the United Kingdom, 6 x 6

JS2013.527.40

Encaustic tile depicting symbols associated with the Earl of Shrewsbury, designed by A.W.N. Pugin, Minton & Co., c.1840, 6 x 6

JS2013.527.41

From St Mary's Convent, Birmingham.

Encaustic tile depicting symbols associated with the Earl of Shrewsbury, designed by A.W.N. Pugin, Minton & Co., c.1840, 6 x 6

JS2013.527.48

From St Mary's Convent, Birmingham.

Right: Encaustic tiles, Boch Frères Maubeuge, Belgium, c.1880, 6½ x 6½

JS2013.527.59, JS2013.527.58

Part of the picture of Viollet-le-Duc's howling hounds panel? I have no grounds for this attribution save 'feel'; the French maestro greatly influenced Pugin in his perusal of the Gothic across the channel. So till proven otherwise let's call it Viollet-le-Duc! I would hope that tile students or anyone with an enquiring spirit will try to fill the gaps or correct mistakes in my collection.

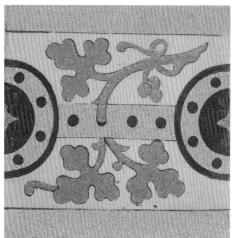

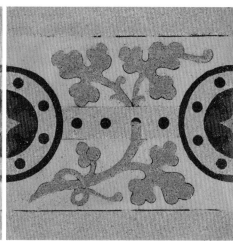

Right: Relief-moulded majolica tiles, Minton & Co., 1860–1870, 6 x 6

JS2013.527.49, JS2013.527.51, JS2013.527.55, JS2013.527.56, JS2013.527.50, JS2013.527.57

Below: Encaustic tiles, Maw & Co., c.1880, 6 x 6

JS2013.527.53, JS2013.527.54, JS2013.527.52

153

Glazed encaustic tile, Robert Minton Taylor & Co., c.1871, 6 x 6

JS2013.527.68

Anything with an anthemion!

Encaustic tiles, Boch Frères Maubeuge, Belgium, c.1880, 6½ x 6½

JS2013.527.61, JS2013.527.63, JS2013.527.60, JS2013.527.62

Entrancing design, probably Viollet-le-Duc, a considerable influence on A.W.N. Pugin.

Encaustic tiles, Minton & Co., 1866, 6 x 6

JS2013.527.66, JS2013.527.64, JS2013.527.67, JS2013.527.65

Certainly by Pugin but whether father or son? When I see SANCTUS proclaimed I always think of Antonio Gaudi and his Sagrada Familia. SANCTUS is splashed in ceramic at high level on Gaudi's unfinished Catalan masterpiece.

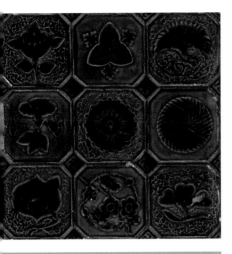

Relief-moulded tile, The Campbell Brick & Tile Co., c.1875, 6 x 6

JS2013.527.70

Block-printed tile, Maw & Co., c.1930, 6 x 6

JS2013.527.71

Block-printed tile, Minton & Co., 6 x 6

JS2013.527.73

Transfer-printed tile, Wedgwood, c.1890, 6 x 6

JS2013.527.69

Just a pretty pattern – William Morrisesque.

Block-printed tile, 6 x 6

JS2013.527.72

Transfer-printed tile, Minton China Works, 6 x 6

JS2013.527.74

I'm always attracted to good tiles of Japanese influence.

Transfer-printed tile, Webbs Tileries, Worcester, 1870–1900, 6 x 6

JS2013.527.75

Block-printed tile, Minton China Works, 6 x 6

JS2013.527.76

Acquired through a swap with Keith Horie in exchange for some cast-iron with which he wanted to enrich his home, Fernbank.

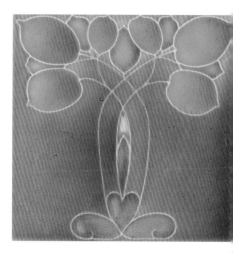

Tube-lined Art Nouveau tile, Minton Hollins & Co., c.1910, 6 x 6

JS2013.527.77

Still the attraction of Art Nouveau lingers.

Block-printed and hand-painted tile, designed by A.W.N. Pugin, Minton Hollins & Co., c.1880, 6 x 6

JS2013.527.78

Block-printed tile, Minton Hollins & Co., 1875–1910, 6 x 6

JS2013.527.79

Transfer-printed tile, Pilkington & Carter Tiles Ltd, 1966, 6 x 6

JS2013.527.81

I suspect inspired by Australian Aboriginal art which has become very popular recently.

Transfer-printed tile depicting Corfe Castle, Dorset, designed by Bernard Charles, Carter & Co., 1960s, 6 x 6

JS2013.527.82

Block-printed tile, Minton China Works, 8 x 8

JS2013.527.86

Much influenced by similar pavement in the ruins of Pompeii or London excavations.

Hand-painted tile depicting the nursery rhyme Jack and Jill, amateur copy of a Walter Crane design on a Minton Hollins & Co. blank, 8 x 8

JS2013.527.87

Transfer-printed tile, designed by Peggy Angus, Pilkington & Carter Tiles Ltd, 1967, 6 x 6

JS2013.527.83

Very nice geometric with fine colour toning.

Encaustic tile panel, W. Godwin, 11½ x 11½

JS2013.527.85

Encaustic tile, Minton & Co., c.1880, 12 x 12

JS2013.527.84

The Christian fish symbol.

Relief-moulded tile, Minton Hollins & Co.,
8 x 8

JS2013.527.88

From Andy Tilbrook. Excellent Minton
Hollins.

Block-printed tile, Minton & Co., 8 x 7½

JS2013.527.89

Block-printed tile, Minton & Co., 8 x 8

JS2013.527.90

Dresseresque in style.

Block-printed tile, designed by Walter Crane, Maw & Co., c.1880, 8 x 8

JS2013.527.91

A classical design.

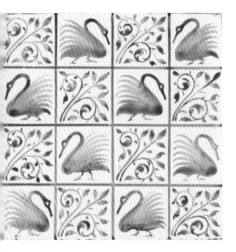

Hand-painted tile, Swan design by Philip Webb, 1860s, 6 x 6

JS2013.527.196

Encaustic tile, Minton & Co., 1871, 6 x 6

JS2013.527.136

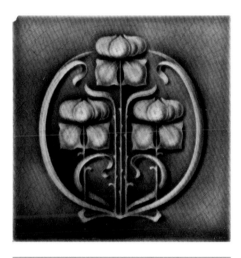

Relief-moulded Art Nouveau tile, c.1910, 6 x 6

JS2013.527.137

Encaustic tile with colour glazed inlay,
early Minton, 6 x 6

JS2013.527.134

Richard Coeur de Lion off to the Crusades.

Encaustic tiles, designed by John Pollard
Seddon, Maw & Co., c.1880, 4 x 4

**JS2013.527.37, JS2013.527.117, JS2013.527.115,
JS2013.527.116**

Hand-painted tile, William De Morgan,
6 x 6

JS2013.527.118

Islamic inspiration.

Hand-painted tile, Daisy design by William
Morris, c.1860s, 6 x 6

JS2013.527.119

A gift from Michael Whiteway for providing
two weeks' accommodation at Westbourne
Grove, whilst a squatter occupied his flat in
Holland Villas Road, W14.

Hand-painted tile, Bough design by William
Morris, 1860s, 5 x 5

JS2013.527.120

Encaustic tile, Minton & Co., 8 diameter

JS2013.527.122

A likely Minton spare from the Palace of Westminster.

Block-printed gold lustre tile, Minton Hollins & Co., 1875–1910, 6 x 6

JS2013.527.121

Very quixotic and kaleidoscopic. Re-focus your eye on different parts of the tile for maximum pleasure.

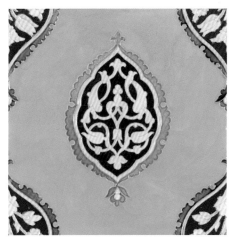

Relief-moulded majolica tile, Minton & Co., c.1880, 8 x 8

JS2013.527.123

Left: Encaustic tiles, Minton & Co., 6 x 6

JS2013.527.124, JS2013.527.125

Two sides of a panel of four. I'm still awaiting the other tiles!

Encaustic tiles, Chamberlain & Co., Worcester, 6 x 3

JS2013.527.185, JS2013.527.184

161

Encaustic border tile, 'M' for 'Maria', designed by A.W.N. Pugin, Minton & Co., c.1840, 6 x 6

JS2013.527.126

Originally from St Peter's Church, Marlow. The tiles were distributed amongst the congregation when the church was demolished. A beautiful Pugin design.

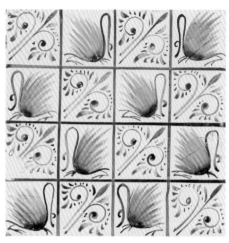

Hand-painted tile, Swan design by William Morris, 1860s, 5 x 5

JS2013.527.127

Relief-moulded majolica glazed tile, Minton & Co., 6 x 6

JS2013.527.177

From my very good friend Bob Smith of Leicester with chip in corner. A superb tile.

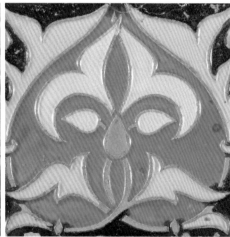

Left: Relief-moulded majolica tiles, designed by A.W.N. Pugin for the Great Exhibition, Minton & Co., 1851, 5 x 5

JS2013.527.129, JS2013.527.130

Islamic style.

Hand-painted tile by Majel Davidson, J.C. Edwards (Ruabon) blank, 1920s, 6 x 6

JS2013.527.133

Encaustic tile, Minton & Co., 1863, 6 x 6

JS2013.527.178

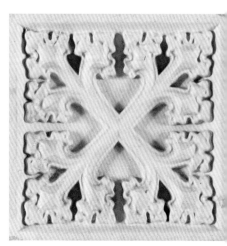

Relief-moulded tile, 5¾ x 5¾

JS2013.527.179

Encaustic tiles, W. Godwin, 6 x 6

JS2013.527.131, JS2013.527.132, JS2013.527.135,
JS2013.527.128

Glazed encaustic tile, Maw & Co., 6 x 3

JS2013.527.182

Encaustic tile, Maw & Co., 6 x 6

JS2013.527.180

Encaustic tile, Chamberlain & Co.,
Worcester, 5⅞ x 5⅞

JS2013.527.181

163

'The Lady from Hereford Hoard' acquired
by Mr Neal Phillips. It sounds grand but her
huge pile of Godwin tiles had, no doubt, a
humble and mundane source. They were
mostly covered in cement and so I spent
many happy hours with my hand grinder!

These tiles make me reflect on Jon
Catleugh's De Morgan dream: to acquire
each one of his designs. Impossible to
collect all the English tiles made between
1830 and 1930 with all that myriad of tiny
factories and workshops – just a day dream.

Encaustic tile, W. Godwin, 6 x 6

JS2013.527.194

fabulous product.

Encaustic tile, W. Godwin, 6 x 6

JS2013.527.195

Encaustic tile, 4 x 4

JS2013.527.251

Perhaps I should have cut down my collection as the number of encaustic tiles made between 1830 and 1920 are as numerous as the sands on the sea shore – or so it seems!

Encaustic tile, W. Godwin, 4 x 4

JS2013.527.227

Good design.

Glazed encaustic tile, Craven Dunnill & Co., 4 x 4

JS2013.527.225

Lovely encaustic *Fleur-de-Lys*.

Encaustic tile, Minton Hollins & Co., 4 x 4

JS2013.527.226

Encaustic tile, Maw & Co., 4 x 4

JS2013.527.223

John Pollard Seddon.

Encaustic tile, W. Godwin, 4 x 4

JS2013.527.224

Copy of a medieval design.

Encaustic tiles, Maw & Co., 4 x 4

JS2013.527.215, JS2013.527.214, JS2013.527.216, JS2013.527.213

Arrestingly attractive.

Right: Encaustic tiles, designed by John Pollard Seddon, Maw & Co., 4 x 4

JS2013.527.222, JS2013.527.221, JS2013.527.220, JS2013.527.219

He made many designs with varied colourways and in different sizes.

Left: Part-glazed, red-bodied relief-moulded tile, Maw & Co., 4 x 4

JS2013.527.217

Bought from the John Stevens cache at 87 Hammersmith Grove.

Encaustic border tile, Craven Dunnill & Co., 1871–1900, 6 x 1½

JS2013.527.228

Encaustic tile, Maw & Co., 4 x 4

JS2013.527.218

Designed by John Pollard Seddon.

Encaustic tile, Maw & Co., 4 x 4

JS2013.527.230

Encaustic tile, Maw & Co., 4 x 4

JS2013.527.229

Encaustic tile, Maw & Co., 4 x 4

JS2013.527.234

Glazed encaustic tile, Minton & Co., 6 x 6

JS2013.527.231

Glazed encaustic tile, W. Godwin, 4 x 4

JS2013.527.232

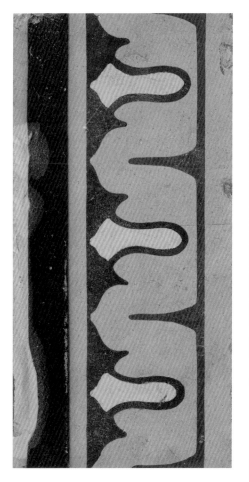

Glazed encaustic tile, Maw & Co., 6 x 4

JS2013.527.205

Very beautiful 'Dresseresque' design.

Encaustic border tile, Minton & Co.,
5½ x 5½

JS2013.527.210

Below: Printed outline and hand-coloured
landscape from the 'New Domesday Book
of Kent' series, designed by Donald
Maxwell, Doulton, 1935, 4 x 4

JS2013.527.209

I like them as they remind me of Rowland
Hilder. As a schoolboy in 1949, I hung a
print of his on my wall.

Relief-moulded tile, Craven Dunnill & Co.,
1880–1910, 3 x 3

JS2013.527.233

Encaustic tile, W. Godwin, 4 x 4

JS2013.527.212

Four tiles would make a stunning impact.

Encaustic tile, Boch Frères Maubeuge, Belgium, c.1880, 6½ x 6½

JS2013.527.198

The damage to the surface illustrates the depth of the inlay and coarse mix of the colours as opposed to the fine colours and surface of Minton. I sense a Viollet-le-Duc design, a great French Gothic Revivalist who inspired Pugin. Tile knowledge is expanded by someone who can prove me wrong. I welcome comments and controversy.

Glazed encaustic tiles, W. Godwin, 4 x 4

JS2013.527.206, JS2013.527.207

Hand-painted tile, William Morris, 1860s, 5 x 5

JS2013.527.208

Tube-lined tile, Samian Ware, Malkin Tiles Ltd, c.1930, 4 x 4

JS2013.527.211

Left: Glazed encaustic tiles, W. Godwin, 6 x 6

JS2013.527.201, JS2013.527.204, JS2013.527.202, JS2013.527.203

Glazed encaustic, Minton Hollins & Co., 1868, 4 x 4

JS2013.527.199

Fine design. Note the 'wireless cloisonné' effect on the green leaves.

Encaustic tiles, Craven Dunnill & Co., 5 x 5

JS2013.527.275, JS2013.527.274, JS2013.527.276, JS2013.527.273

These are inspired by ancient images of the Green Man or the Devil. He fits excellently in the corner of a tile – rich lovely glaze.

Right: Glazed encaustic tile, Maw & Co., 6 x 6

JS2013.527.197

In my Top Fifty.

Glazed encaustic tile, W. Godwin, 4 x 4

JS2013.527.200

Exquisitely crafted.

Hand-painted tile by John Scott's mother, Ada Vera Marshall, in 1955 on a Rako blank, 6 x 6

JS2013.527.340

This is part of my college crest – Corpus Christi College, Oxford.

Transfer-printed tile, Copeland, 6 x 6

JS2013.527.341

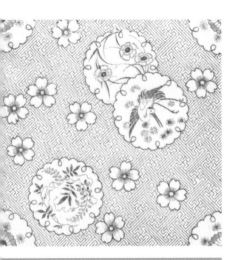

Transfer-printed tile, Minton China Works, 6 x 6

JS2013.527.344

Block-printed tile, Minton China Works, 1868–1900, 6 x 6

JS2013.527.343

Screen-printed tile, designed by Laurence Scarfe, Carter & Co., 1968, 6 x 6

JS2013.527.342

Nice strong modern design. Expressive of the 60s.

Transfer-printed tile, Copeland, 6 x 6

JS2013.527.345

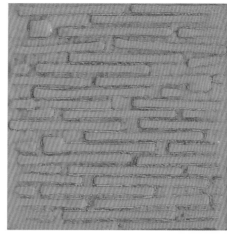

Hand-painted tile, Malkin Johnson Tiles,
1963–1975, 6 x 6

JS2013.527.346

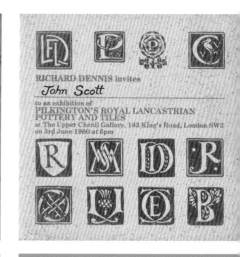

Exhibition invitation tile, 6 x 6

JS2013.527.347

Richard Dennis exhibition invitation.

Imitation mosaic, Minton China Works,
6 x 6

JS2013.527.348

Encaustic tile, Minton & Co., 6 x 6

JS2013.527.349

Screen-printed and hand-painted tile,
designed by Peggy Angus, Carter & Co.,
1950s, 6 x 6

JS2013.527.351

Screen-printed tiles, designed by Laurence
Scarfe, Carter & Co., c.1963, 6 x 6

JS2013.527.352, JS2013.527.350

Encaustic tile, The Campbell Brick & Tile
Co., 1875–1882, 6 x 6

JS2013.527.379

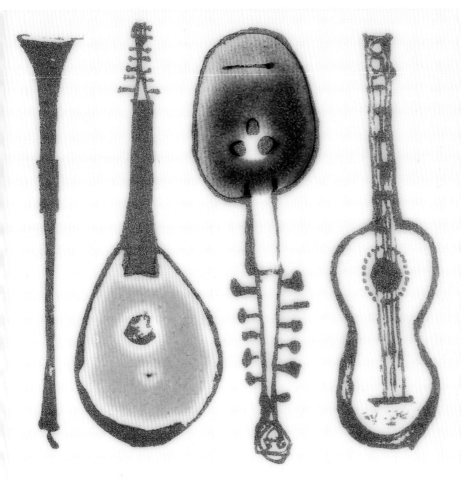

Encaustic tile, Minton & Co., 6 x 6

JS2013.527.380

Hand screen-printed wax resist tile, Mandolins design by Ann Clark, pattern no. 62, H. & R. Johnson blank, 1959, 6 x 6

JS2013.527.353

I began by collecting 18th-century objects – what a snob I was! It has taken a long time to admire contemporary things. But Ann is a heroine of this genre. She has a fabulous eye and hand.

Encaustic tiles, W. Godwin, 6 x 6

JS2013.527.384, JS2013.527.387

These Godwin geometric encaustic tiles are particularly attractive. The surface is distressed, I believe purposefully, to achieve a lovely comfortable worn aspect. With zestful cleaning and much 'spit and polish' the surface becomes delightfully antique.

Relief-moulded tile, The Campbell Brick & Tile Co., 1875–1882, 6 x 6

JS2013.527.378

Hand-painted tile, designed by Alfred Read, Carter & Co., 1950s, 6 x 6

JS2013.527.382

Encaustic tile, W. Godwin, 6 x 6

JS2013.527.383

Note the distressed finish and shield to impress the neighbours with the antiquity of your domain!

Relief-moulded tile, Pilkington, 6 x 6

JS2013.527.381

Encaustic tile, W. Godwin, 6 x 6

JS2013.527.385

Encaustic tile, W. Godwin, 6 x 6

JS2013.527.386

Encaustic tile, W. Godwin, 6 x 6

JS2013.527.388

Note the glorious uneven surface so ennobled by a good wax polish. In my Top Twenty-five.

Encaustic tile, Chamberlain & Co., 1840–1848, 6 x 3

JS2013.527.339

Design inspired by the medieval.

Encaustic tile, W. Godwin, 4 x 4

JS2013.527.389

Encaustic tile, 4 x 4

JS2013.527.390

Encaustic tile, W. Godwin, 5 x 5

JS2013.527.391

Encaustic tile, W. Godwin, 4 x 4

JS2013.527.392

Encaustic tile, St George's Tile Works, 4 x 4

JS2013.527.393

Encaustic tiles, W. Godwin, 5 x 5

JS2013.527.394, JS2013.527.395

Fanciful heraldry.

Left: Encaustic tile, Minton & Co., 6 x 4

JS2013.527.396

Design inspired by the medieval.

Left: Encaustic tiles, Minton & Co., 6 x 6

JS2013.527.397, JS2013.527.398, JS2013.527.399, JS2013.527.400

This panel is a delight. What a joy it would be to walk on such a pavement! In my Top Fifty.

Right: Encaustic tiles, Minton & Co., 6 x 6

JS2013.527.402, JS2013.527.401, JS2013.527.404, JS2013.527.403

I find this hypnotically absorbing. My eye can create a million squares large and small, upwards & sideways … never bored.
In my Top Thirty-five.

Over-glaze enamelled tiles, designed by
A.W.N. Pugin, Minton & Co., 1842–1845,
6 x 6

JS2013.527.408, JS2013.527.407, JS2013.527.406,
JS2013.527.405

Timelessly popular.

Relief-moulded tile, Craven Dunnill & Co., 3 x 3

JS2013.527.584

Encaustic tiles, Minton & Co., 6 x 6

JS2013.527.409, JS2013.527.410, JS2013.527.411, JS2013.527.412

An enthralling design which was produced in many colourways. On reflection it would be much improved with a pattern of nine.

Encaustic tile, Maw & Co., 4¼ x 4¼

JS2013.527.585

Encaustic border tile, 6 x 1½

JS2013.527.582

Encaustic border tile, 6 x 1½

JS2013.527.583

Right: Encaustic border tile, Maw & Co.,
6 x 3

JS2013.527.580

Encaustic border tile, Craven Dunnill & Co.,
6 x 3

JS2013.527.581

Encaustic tile, Minton & Co., 6 x 6

JS2013.527.566

Relief-moulded tile, Maw & Co., 6 x 4

JS2013.527.579

Relief-moulded tile, Maw & Co., 6 x 4

JS2013.527.578

Encaustic tile, W. Godwin, 6 x 6

JS2013.527.567

Encaustic tile, W. Godwin, 6 x 6

JS2013.527.565

Encaustic tile, W. Godwin, 6 x 6

JS2013.527.574

Silk-screen printed tile, designed by Polly Brace for Dunsmore Tiles, George Woolliscroft & Sons blank, 6 x 6

JS2013.527.575

Encaustic tile, W. Godwin, 6 x 6

JS2013.527.564

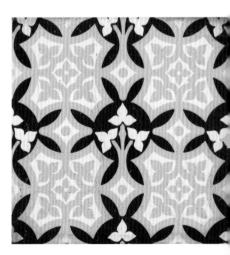

Encaustic tile, Minton & Co., 6 x 6

JS2013.527.572

Glazed encaustic tile, W. Godwin, 6 x 6

JS2013.527.568

Glazed encaustic tile, W. Godwin, 6 x 6

JS2013.527.569

Glazed encaustic tile, W. Godwin, 6 x 6

JS2013.527.571

Glazed encaustic tile, W. Godwin, 6 x 6

JS2013.527.570

Glazed encaustic tile, W. Godwin, 6 x 6

JS2013.527.573

Glazed encaustic tile, W. Godwin, 5 x 5

JS2013.527.587

Glazed encaustic border tile, Craven Dunnill & Co., 5 x 5

JS2013.527.586

Encaustic tile, W. Godwin, 6 x 6

JS2013.527.836

A charmingly worn tile.

Encaustic tile, Minton & Co., 1862, 6 x 6

JS2013.527.837

Glazed encaustic tile, W. Godwin, 6 x 6

JS2013.527.838

Glazed encaustic tile, 6 x 6

JS2013.527.839

Encaustic tile, The Campbell Brick & Tile Co., 6 x 6

JS2013.527.840

Encaustic tile, Minton & Co., 6 x 6

JS2013.527.841

Glazed encaustic tile, W. Godwin, 6 x 6

JS2013.527.842

Relief-moulded tile, 6 x 6

JS2013.527.844

Encaustic tiles, Minton & Co., 6 x 6

JS2013.527.846, JS2013.527.845

Please find the other two!

Encaustic tile, Robert Minton Taylor, 1870s, 6 x 6

JS2013.527.843

Encaustic tile, Minton & Co., 1867, 6 x 6

JS2013.527.847

Glazed encaustic tile, W. Godwin, 6 x 6

JS2013.527.848

Glazed encaustic tile, W. Godwin, 6 x 6

JS2013.527.849

Glazed encaustic tile, W. Godwin, 6 x 6

JS2013.527.850

Glazed encaustic tile, W. Godwin, 6 x 6

JS2013.527.851

A most common two-colour Godwin.

Encaustic tile, Minton & Co., 6 x 6

JS2013.527.852

Glazed encaustic tile, The Campbell Brick & Tile Co., 6 x 6

JS2013.527.871

Encaustic tile, Minton & Co., 6 x 6

JS2013.527.873

Great design achieved with apparent simplicity.

Encaustic tile, Minton & Co., 6 x 6

JS2013.527.874

Encaustic tile, W. Godwin, 6 x 6

JS2013.527.872

Encaustic tile, Robert Minton Taylor & Co., 1871–1874, 6 x 6

JS2013.527.869

Glazed encaustic tile, Minton & Co., 1879, 6 x 6

JS2013.527.870

Glazed encaustic tile, Minton & Co., 6 x 6

JS2013.527.866

Glazed encaustic tile, W. Godwin, 6 x 6

JS2013.527.865

Left: Glazed encaustic tile, W. Godwin, 6 x 6

JS2013.527.868

Glazed encaustic tile, Minton & Co., 6 x 6

JS2013.527.867

Encaustic tile, Maw & Co., 6 x 6

JS2013.527.859

Glazed encaustic tile, Robert Minton Taylor & Co., 1871–1874, 6 x 6

JS2013.527.860

A strong and masterful design, for a fish shop?

Relief-moulded tile, Maw & Co., 6 x 6

JS2013.527.861

An architectural 'feel'.

Glazed encaustic tile, Minton & Co., 6 x 6

JS2013.527.862

Encaustic tile, from the Palace of Westminster, Minton & Co., 6 x 6

JS2013.527.863

Encaustic tile, Minton & Co., 6 x 6

JS2013.527.864

Encaustic tile, Craven Dunnill & Co., 6 x 6

JS2013.527.1157

Said to be from the burnt-out basement of one of the Inns of Court.

Encaustic tile, Minton & Co., 6 x 6

JS2013.527.1158

Relief-moulded majolica glazed tile, The Campbell Brick & Tile Co., 1876, 6 x 6

JS2013.527.1159

Very beautiful border tile – a feast for the eyes.

Encaustic tile from Downton Castle. The monogram refers to Andrew Rouse Boughton Knight whose extensions to the estate buildings in the 1860s included these tiles made by Minton & Co., c.1860, 6 x 6

JS2013.527.1160

Encaustic tile, Minton & Co., 6 x 6

JS2013.527.1163

Glazed encaustic tile, W. Godwin, 6 x 6

JS2013.527.1164

Block-printed tile, possibly designed by Owen Jones, Maw & Co., 6 x 6

JS2013.527.1143

Exquisite anthemion design. In my Top Thirty.

Block-printed tile, Maw & Co., 6 x 6

JS2013.527.1144

Block-printed tile, Minton China Works, 6 x 6

JS2013.527.1145

Very fine. Owen Jones or Dresser. In my Top Twenty-five.

Encaustic tile, Webb Tileries, 6 x 6

JS2013.527.1146

Nothing very special – just a little fodder for a fanatic on a Saturday at Portobello Market.

Encaustic tile, Minton & Co., c.1850, 6 x 6

JS2013.527.1147

I thought I would keep this forever, waiting for the other three! Then after 20 years a full set came along.

Encaustic tile, Maw & Co., 6 x 6

JS2013.527.1148

Encaustic tile, Maw & Co., 6 x 6

JS2013.527.1149

Encaustic tile, W. Godwin, 6 x 6

JS2013.527.1150

Encaustic tile, W. Godwin, 6 x 6

JS2013.527.1151

Encaustic tile, Minton & Co., 6 x 6

JS2013.527.1153

Encaustic tile, Minton & Co., 6 x 6

JS2013.527.1152

Block-printed tile, Minton China Works, 6 x 6

JS2013.527.1154

Encaustic tile, 6 x 6

JS2013.527.1155

Encaustic tile, The Campbell Brick & Tile Co., 6 x 6

JS2013.527.1161

Encaustic tile, 6 x 6

JS2013.527.1156

Encaustic tile, Minton & Co., 6 x 6

JS2013.527.1162

This is a very common mid-19th-century design. I note it is extensively used in George Edmund Street's Law Courts in the Strand. Did Street design these? Almost certainly not. He would have chosen a suitable example from a Minton pattern book – as so many others did throughout Great Britain and the Empire.

Right: Glazed encaustic tile, W. Godwin, 6 x 6

JS2013.527.1165

Glazed encaustic tile, Craven Dunnill & Co., 6 x 6

JS2013.527.1167

Glazed encaustic tile, Maw & Co., 6 x 6

JS2013.527.1168

Glazed encaustic tile, Minton & Co., 6 x 6

JS2013.527.1170

Anyone who finds the owner of this coat of arms deserves a prize. It was probably manufactured to impress the neighbours!

Glazed encaustic tile, Minton & Co., 1864, 6 x 6

JS2013.527.1166

Glazed encaustic tiles, W. Godwin, 6 x 6

JS2013.527.1171, JS2013.527.1172

I have no hesitation in coupling odd colourways as long as the design is the same. A great design which comes in many colourways.

Glazed encaustic tile, Minton & Co., 6 x 6

JS2013.527.1169

Made for a fruit shop? Certainly a thing of beauty. With moderate care, it will last forever.

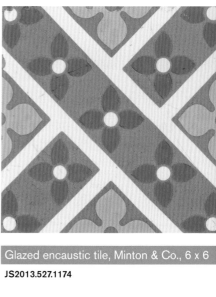

Glazed encaustic tile, Minton & Co., 6 x 6

JS2013.527.1174

Glazed encaustic tile, Minton & Co., 6 x 6

JS2013.527.1173

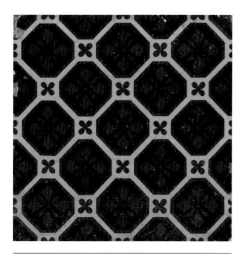

Glazed encaustic tile, Minton & Co., 6 x 6

JS2013.527.1175

Glazed encaustic tile, Minton & Co., 6 x 6

JS2013.527.1176

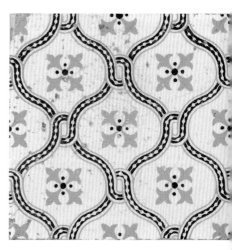

Glazed encaustic tile, Minton & Co., 6 x 6

JS2013.527.1177

Relief-moulded tile, Minton Hollins & Co.,
6 x 6

JS2013.527.1217

Relief-moulded majolica tile, Minton & Co.,
7 x 7

JS2013.527.1218

Very decorative. In my Top 100.

Glazed encaustic tile, Minton & Co., 6 x 6

JS2013.527.1178

Glazed encaustic tile, W. Godwin, 6 x 6

JS2013.527.1179

Encaustic tile, W. Godwin, 5¾ x 5¾

JS2013.527.1180

Hand-painted tiles from the 'Animal' series,
pattern no. A3, designed by Rosalind
Ord for Packard & Ord on a Rhodes Tile
Co. blank, c.1935, 6 x 6

JS2013.527.1215, JS2013.527.1216

Left: Encaustic tiles, Maw & Co., 6 x 6

JS2013.527.1212, JS2013.527.1211

Such a lovely design. Two is better than one
In my Top 100.

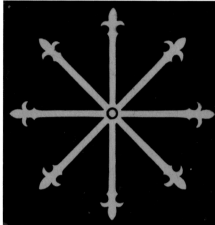

Glazed encaustic tile, Minton & Co., 6 x 6

JS2013.527.1213

Left: Glazed encaustic tile, Minton & Co.,
1871, 6 x 6

JS2013.527.1214

I love these tiles so much I like to have one
always 'to hand' or more accurately 'to eye'!

Left: Encaustic tiles, Minton & Co., 7 x 7
JS2013.527.1207, JS2013.527.1208, JS2013.527.1210,
JS2013.527.1209

Right: Glazed encaustic tiles, Webb
Tileries, 6 x 6

JS2013.527.1203, JS2013.527.1204, JS2013.527.1205,
JS2013.527.1206

Designed by a master of the anthemion –
what a glorious spread! In my Top Fifty.

Relief-moulded majolica tile, Minton & Co., 6½ x 6½

JS2013.527.1201

Encaustic tile, possibly designed by John Pollard Seddon, W. Godwin, 5¾ x 5¾

JS2013.527.1202

Relief-moulded tile, Doulton, 6 x 6

JS2013.527.1222

Hand-painted tiles, designed by Alistair Macduff, Dorincourt Industries on a Carter & Co. blank, 1956, 6 x 6

JS2013.527.1219, JS2013.527.1220

We tile freaks are lucky indeed to have a most enthusiastic dealer in Adrian Grate, who travels far and wide and has a genuine passion for characterful ceramics. These figures have real zip.

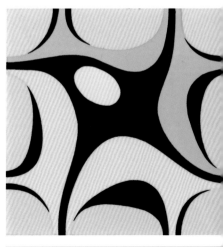

Screen-printed tile, Carter & Co., 1959, 6 x 6

JS2013.527.1221

Abstract expressionism.

Right: Relief-moulded tile, Maw & Co.,
6 x 6

JS2013.527.1223

Evocative of a May Day roundel. A very
beautiful tile.

Transfer-printed tiles, Minton Hollins & Co.,
6 x 6

JS2013.527.1224, JS2013.527.1225, JS2013.527.1226

I suspect these hexagonal tiles lined regal
lavatories. Somewhere I have another set
which probably came from the Duke of
Westminster's earlier home at Eaton Hall.

Right: Transfer-printed tile, Minton
Hollins & Co., 6 x 6

JS2013.527.1227

Hexagonal tile, probably from earlier Victoria
and Albert Museum toilets.

Transfer-printed and hand-painted tile, 8 x 8

JS2013.527.1231

Encaustic tiles, Minton & Co., 8 x 8

JS2013.527.1229, JS2013.527.1230, JS2013.527.1228

I bought these as they were so odd. A real find for a student of the history of child labour. No doubt in time someone will tell the story. Much in need of research!

Encaustic tile, Minton & Co., 1866, 6 x 3

JS2013.527.1258

Encaustic tile, possibly designed by John
Pollard Seddon, Maw & Co., 6 x 6

JS2013.527.1255

Relief-moulded tile, W. Godwin, 4¼ x 4¼

JS2013.527.1260

Encaustic tile with painted inlay, Minton &
Co., c.1840, 5¾ x 5¾

JS2013.527.1261

Slip-trailed tile, J.C. Edwards (Ruabon),
post-1887, 6 x 6

JS2013.527.1262

Transfer-printed and hand-painted tile,
W. Godwin, 5¾ x 5¾

JS2013.527.1263

Relief-moulded tile, Maw & Co., 4 x 6

JS2013.527.1259

Relief-moulded tile, Maw & Co., 6 x 6

JS2013.527.1264

Encaustic tile, 6 x 6

JS2013.527.1265

Encaustic tile, Minton & Co., 5¾ x 5¾

JS2013.527.1266

Encaustic tile, Minton & Co., 5¾ x 5¾

JS2013.527.1269

Encaustic tile, 6 x 6

JS2013.527.1267

Encaustic tile, 6 x 6

JS2013.527.1268

Encaustic tiles, Minton & Co., 6 x 6

JS2013.527.1296, JS2013.527.1295

Awaiting 16 more to make the real picture.

Glazed encaustic tile, W. Godwin, 6 x 6

JS2013.527.1294

Glazed encaustic tile, Minton & Co., 6 x 6

JS2013.527.1293

Glazed encaustic tile, Minton & Co., 6 x 6

JS2013.527.1292

Glazed encaustic tile, W. Godwin, 6 x 6

JS2013.527.1289

Glazed encaustic tile, Minton & Co., 6 x 6

JS2013.527.1290

Opposite: Encaustic tiles from the Palace of Westminster, Minton & Co. These five tiles were arranged by the collector to spell the word 'Queen'. However it appears that several letters have been inverted to enable this spelling.

JS2013.527.1280, JS2013.527.1282, JS2013.527.1283
JS2013.527.1284, JS2013.527.1281

Glazed encaustic, possibly designed by John Pollard Seddon, Maw & Co., 6 x 6

JS2013.527.1285

Encaustic tile, Minton & Co., 6 x 6

JS2013.527.1286

Block-printed pseudo-encaustic tile, Minton China Works, 6 x 6

JS2013.527.1291

Glazed encaustic tiles, W. Godwin, 6 x 6

JS2013.527.1288, JS2013.527.1287

Opposite: Hand-painted faience panel depicting the Fairies at the Christening, Sleeping Beauty by Margaret E. Thompson for Doulton, c.1905, 62 x 50

JS2013.527.1785

A renowned picture panel that was ideal for a hospital children's ward. The original location and the rationale behind its removal are unknown. Impossible to investigate the historic crime of removing such a worthwhile and beautiful part of our heritage.

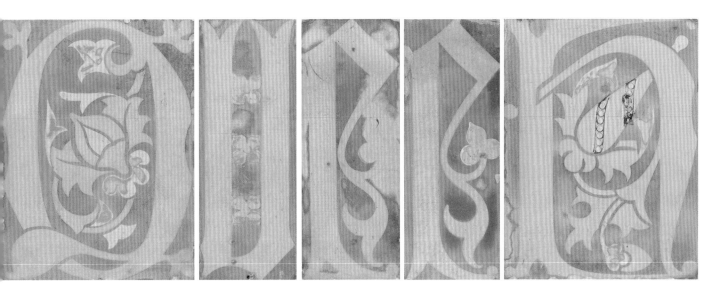

JS2013.527.1763

A wonderful panel. Charles Handley-Read bought one of these and gave it to the V&A. In my Top Five.

Encaustic tile panel, Maw & Co., 32½ x 32½

JS2013.527.1793

This panel is part of a pavement that was removed from a church about to be demolished.

Encaustic tile panel from Southwark Cathedral, designed by A.W.N. Pugin, Minton & Co., 23 x 23

JS2013.527.1787

I was able to buy many of these tiles through Michael Whiteway. Designed by A.W.N. Pugin and used extensively in his other churches including the finest, and his favourite, St Giles, Cheadle. This is a jewel in the crown of the finest decorative art of the age. All the tiles were in poor condition, scarred by war. A must to see.

Hand-painted tile panel, Antelope design by William De Morgan, 1880s, 40½ x 46½

JS2013.527.1766

This was hung in Old Battersea House, a renowned repository for fine Victorian art and particularly rich in De Morgan's work. The panel was broken whilst there. Originally I bought half of the panel and then, years later, I managed to acquire some more of it, although six tiles were missing. I am deeply indebted to David Burnham Smith for his four-year labour of love in recreating those missing tiles. He has now turned his hand to his own sculpture with consummate success. A fabulous image, in my Top Five.

This panel was broken whilst at Old Battersea House. John Scott bought the panel in two pieces and had it restored. The conservator painstakingly matched colours and painting technique to replace six missing tiles. He attached his experimental tiles to the back of the panel.

Encaustic tile panel, Minton & Co., 33 x 33

JS2013.527.1762

Removed by me from the Birch Church,
Manchester. Being encaustic it is very heavy
and awkward to handle but it does show
that you need 4, 6, 8, 10, 16 and sometimes
25 to reveal the whole picture. With a lot
of polish and a little sunshine, the finish is
exquisite. I burst a tyre of my VW Scirocco
carrying this back to London. In my Top
Fifteen.

Tube-lined tile panel, designed by
C.F.A. Voysey, 13 x 49½

JS2013.527.1796

Much more attractive as a panel of 16 than
a single – a trite comment. Lovely above a
picture rail … in the right house. In my Top Ten.

Right: Relief-moulded tile panel, designed
by George Howard Elphick for Turkish
baths in north London, used at Brighton
and elsewhere, Craven Dunnill & Co.,
1902, 30¼ x 46

JS2013.527.1799

A glorious panel of yellow-glazed majolica.
The tile shape neatly fits the design. I have
seen a similar panel, but green, in the
entrance to the Brighton Museum.

Hand-painted tile panel, 20¼ x 44½

JS2013.527.1797

At first I thought it was De Morgan. Now I don't know. Exquisite Anglo-oriental. In my Top Twenty.

Glazed encaustic tile panel, Minton & Co., 12 x 12

JS2013.527.1713

Encaustic tile depicting St Mark, made on the continent, 11 x 11

JS2013.527.1728

Right: Hand-painted tile panel for a hospital, Goosey Goosey Gander by Margaret E. Thompson for Doulton, c.1900, 50 x 23

JS2013.527.1790

Originally hung in a children's ward in Buchanan Hospital, St Leonard's-on-Sea, Hastings, opened in 1908. Margaret Thompson has a style that can be 'read' from across the room. You know which is one of hers at a glance. Disgraceful loss of local history and heritage.

Above: Relief-moulded tile panel, Minton Hollins & Co., 73 x 10

JS2013.527.1764

Right: Glazed encaustic tile panel, W. Godwin, 11 x 11

JS2013.527.1745

Left: Encaustic tile panel, Minton Hollins & Co., 20½ x 12

JS2013.527.1692

Beautifully executed.

Encaustic tile panel, designed by John Pollard Seddon, W. Godwin, 9 x 9

JS2013.527.1743

Strikingly dynamic design.

Glazed encaustic tile panel, W. Godwin, 9 x 9

JS2013.527.1744

Right: Hand-painted over-glaze tile panel, Poppy design by William Morris and hand-painted by May Morris, 1870s, 11 x 21

JS2013.527.1693

Dainty and delicious. In my Top Forty.

**Relief-moulded tile panel, Maw & Co.,
12 x 12**

JS2013.527.1742

In my Top Ten for rich variety of colour,
moulding and depth. This would be
sumptuous in the extreme with candlelight.
A feeling of William Burges.

**Transfer-printed and hand-painted tile panel
from the 'Anacreon' series, designed by
John Moyr Smith, Minton China Works,
9 x 38**

JS2013.527.1778

An aesthetic delight with Dresseresque
furnishings. In my Top Fifty.

Encaustic tile panel, Minton & Co.,
12¾ x 12¾

JS2013.527.1775

Encaustic tile panel, W. Godwin,
12¾ x 12¾

JS2013.527.1776

Glazed encaustic tile panel, Minton & Co.,
12½ x 12½

JS2013.527.1760

Glazed encaustic tile panel, Minton & Co.,
12½ x 12½

JS2013.527.1761

Many quatrefoils evoke contemplation of
our Christian faith and thanks to our Maker.
Victorian tiles are highly symbolic. Strong
and satisfying. In my Top Forty.

Block-printed tile panel, Minton China
Works, 1853, 15¼ x 15¼

JS2013.527.1769

Strongly evocative of the frontispiece of
Wren's City Churches by A.H. Mackmurdo
ARIBA (see also Illustration 5.9 of *The
Age of Art Nouveau* by Maurice Rheims).
Unusual, appealing and secular. In my
Top Fifty.

Glazed encaustic tile panel, W. Godwin,
15 x 15

JS2013.527.1774

Just an appealing design.

Block-printed border tiles and transfer-printed sheep tile from a butcher's shop, designed by William Wise, Minton China Works, 20 x 20

JS2013.527.1756

Originally from an Isle of Man butcher's shop. I bought this unseen on the phone.

Relief-moulded tile panel, Maw & Co., 11 x 11

JS2013.527.1754

A glorious and scintillating Maw & Co. polychrome tile.

Encaustic tile panel, Minton & Co., c.1840, 15 x 15

JS2013.527.1753

Snarling leonine dogs, or savage mythical beasts that need 16 for a full repeat. Semi-distressed surface heavily inspired by the medieval.

Encaustic tile panel, Minton & Co., 13 x 13

JS2013.527.1750

Encaustic tile panel, Minton & Co., 13 x 13

JS2013.527.1748

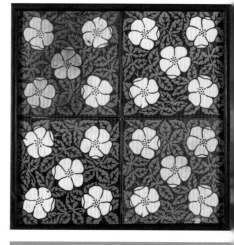

Encaustic tile panel, W. Godwin, 12½ x 12½

JS2013.527.1746

This is one of the rare encaustics that seems substantially secular.

Encaustic tile panel, Minton & Co., 13 x 13

JS2013.527.1716

Christian symbolism.

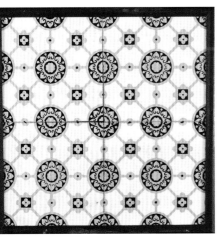

Encaustic tile panel, Minton & Co., 13 x 13

JS2013.527.1717

Encaustic tile panel, Minton & Co., 12 x 12

JS2013.527.1710

Try to design a tile as good as this!

Encaustic tile panel, Minton & Co., 12 x 12

JS2013.527.1715

Encaustic tile panel, The Campbell Brick & Tile Co., 13 x 13

JS2013.527.1709

Left: Encaustic tile panel, Minton & Co., 12½ x 12½

JS2013.527.1708

Think of Pugin returning by train from a day at Cheadle pondering upon the design for Sir Herbert Minton. It is not hard to imagine him 'roughing out' ten such designs in a three-hour journey.

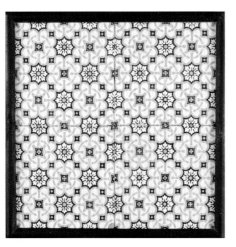

Encaustic tile panel, Minton & Co., 13¼ x 13¼

JS2013.527.1702

Encaustic tile panel, Minton & Co., 12½ x 12½

JS2013.527.1696

Encaustic tile panel, Minton & Co., 13¼ x 13¼

JS2013.527.1695

Left: Encaustic tile panel, Minton & Co., 12½ x 12½

JS2013.527.1703

How many different squares and triangles can your eye construct? The eye never tires of such a game. The interplay of geometric squares and triangles is endlessly fascinating.

Hand-painted tile panel, William De Morgan, 1882–1888, 16 x 5½

JS2013.527.1524

Encaustic tile panel, Minton & Co., 15 x 21

JS2013.527.1512

See Minton's *Old English Tile Design*, 1842 and page 18 of Julian Barnard's *Victorian Ceramic Tiles*. Also on view in Westminster Abbey Chapter House. Copied from/inspired by the medieval.

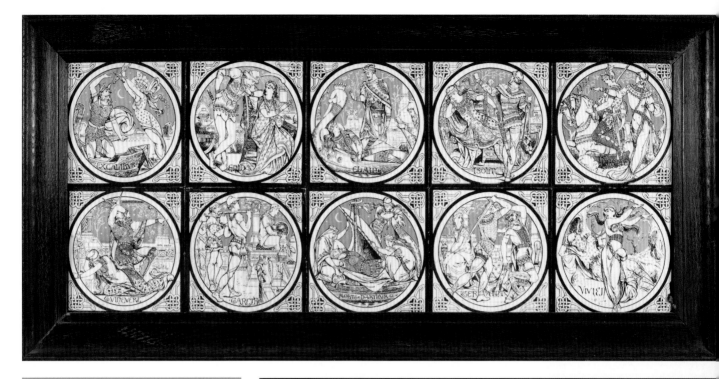

JS2013.527.1740

I always thought I should have a few Moyr Smith tiles. He worked as an assistant in Dr Christopher Dresser's studio and designed numerous sets of highly decorative and stylish historical scenes and fables. Controversy remains over the extent of the work of master and assistant. It is safe to say that Moyr Smith gained valuable experience whilst he worked with Dresser.

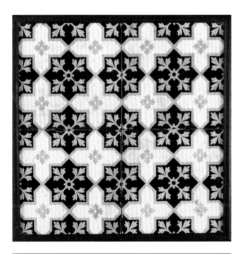

JS2013.527.1632

JS2013.527.1628

Encaustic tile panel, Minton Hollins & Co.,
12¾ x 12¾

JS2013.527.1631

Excellent. Pondering my descriptions of
Victorian encaustic tiles, I wonder, do I
ever see a poor or disastrous design?
Miraculously, I almost never do.

Encaustic tile panel, Minton & Co.,
12½ x 12½

JS2013.527.1633

Relief-moulded tile panel designed by
Lewis F. Day, 27½ x 9½

JS2013.527.1733

Highly natural and pretty.

Hand-painted over-glaze tile panel, peony
design attributed to Kate Faulkner, Morris
& Co., 1880s, 15 x 21

JS2013.527.1618

Transfer-printed tile panel for a butcher's
shop, designed by William Wise, Minton
China Works, 24 x 24

JS2013.527.1509

William Wise places animals in their
environment with such panache. From a
butcher's shop in Douglas, Isle of Man. Wise
was a wizard with figures and farm animals.
Much used in shops, these should be
protected from rapacious developers.

Relief-moulded majolica tile panel, Minton & Co., 10 x 27½

JS2013.527.1613

Beautiful border. Jewel-like aspect. A great favourite of mine. The Queen could not have a more gorgeous top for a favourite sideboard. In my Top Twenty.

Block-printed tile panel, Minton China Works, 11½ x 19½

JS2013.527.1609

Hand-painted tile panel, William De Morgan, 6½ x 13

JS2013.527.1602

Encaustic tile panel, W. Godwin, 12½ x 12½

JS2013.527.1720

Encaustic tile panel, W. Godwin, 12½ x 12½

JS2013.527.1722

Hand-painted tile panel from the 'Shakespearian Characters' series, Packard & Ord Ltd, 1950s, 15 x 15

JS2013.527.1599

Encaustic tile panel, 16 x 16

JS2013.527.1597

A glorious pattern very much inspired by A.W.N. Pugin and probably designed by Christopher Dresser. Stuart Durant, the expert on Dresser, was much enamoured by this and I had to swap a large number of tiles to persuade him to part with these.

JS2013.527.1590

When I found these nine at a salvage fair I
was thrilled. John Wadsworth of Minton is
our best Art Nouveau artist. Intensely clever,
the repeat is achieved with only one tile.
Utterly mesmerising! I've had two of this set
for 25 years and suddenly I found seven
more. I have only seen two other patterns
by Wadsworth but this is the very best.
Wadsworth is so very English – classically
symmetrical, restrained and yet there is
such a mysterious sinuosity! Fabulous!
In my Top Five.

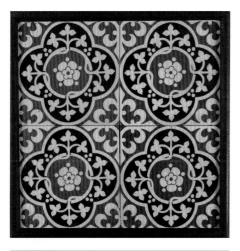

Encaustic tile panel, Minton & Co., 13 x 13

JS2013.527.1704

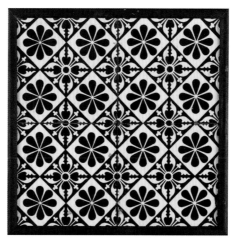

Encaustic tile panel, Minton & Co., 12½ x 12½

JS2013.527.1723

Encaustic tile panel, Minton & Co., 12 x 12

JS2013.527.1719

Encaustic tile panel, Minton & Co., 1871, 13 x 13

JS2013.527.1705

Right: Hand-painted tile panel, designed by William Morris, Morris & Co., 1870–1875, 14½ x 20½

JS2013.527.1689

Obviously more attractive as a panel.

Hand-painted tile panel, William De Morgan, 13 x 19

JS2013.527.1672

Exotic Persian inspiration.

Transfer-printed tiles, designed by Christopher Dresser, Minton Hollins & Co., 1873, 20¼ x 20¼

JS2013.527.1555

Admire the tasteful care reserved for the borders.

Block-printed border tiles and transfer-printed central tile from a butcher's shop, designed by William Wise, Minton China Works, 19½ x 19½

JS2013.527.1592

From a butcher's shop in Douglas, Isle of Man. Border tiles in Greek Key pattern add to the impact.

Encaustic tile panel, Minton & Co., 12 x 12

JS2013.527.1721

The interplay of geometric squares and triangles is outstandingly fascinating. How many squares can your eye fabricate here?

Encaustic tile panel, The Campbell Brick & Tile Co., 13 x 13

JS2013.527.1725

From 'The Chase' series, designed by
Edward Bawden, Carter & Co., 1930s,
8 x 14

JS2013.527.1669

Block-printed tile panel, Minton Hollins &
Co., 11½ x 28

JS2013.527.1687

Left: Designed by Walter Crane, Maw &
Co., 12½ x 24½

JS2013.527.1688

I believe this would have been termed an
archaic design; certainly a far cry from
the glamorous and zestful designs of the
modern master – Dr Christopher Dresser!

Hand-painted tile panel, designed for W.H. Smith, Carter & Co., c.1930, 7¾ x 19

JS2013.527.1691

We hope that the designer of this fascinating panel will be discovered.

Left: Hand-painted tile, William De Morgan, 19 x 6½

JS2013.527.1690

I find the placement of the peacock, its head, body and tail very attractively juxtaposed with the wall and lizards. This is an important quality in the art of tile design, demonstrated vividly by De Morgan who was considered England's greatest tile maker and designer of his day.

Tile panels for a fireplace, designed by Owen Gibbons, Maw & Co., 1880, 9¼ x 27, 27½ x 9½.

JS2013.527.1612, JS2013.527.1685, JS2013.527.1686

Encaustic tile, designed by Christopher Dresser, Minton & Co., 11 x 11

JS2013.527.1637

Christopher Dresser designed this for Bilton Grange in Warwickshire.

Block-printed and hand-coloured tile, designed by A.W.N. Pugin, Minton & Co., 11 x 11

JS2013.527.1635

Encaustic tile from bomb-damaged Southwark Cathedral, designed by A.W.N. Pugin, Minton & Co., 10½ x 10½

JS2013.527.1654

Encaustic tile depicting St Mark, possibly designed by A.W.N. Pugin, Minton & Co., 8½ x 8½

JS2013.527.1659

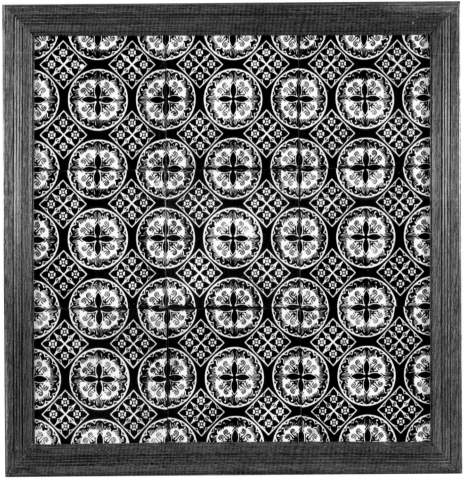

Encaustic tile panel, Minton & Co., 1871, 20½ x 20½

JS2013.527.1549

This was removed from Caldecote Hall, Rutland, which was built in 1875.
A magnificent panel. Probably by Dresser.

Hand-painted tile, William De Morgan, 1898, 8 x 8

JS2013.527.1647

These tiles are at the peak of excellence among English decorative tiles. De Morgan was expert in lustre glaze. He had a zest for the strange and quixotic.

Right: Possibly designed by A.W.N. Pugin, Minton & Co., 10¾ x 10¾

JS2013.527.1636

An exquisite image by Minton, the design inspired by antique examples. Bought from the tile expert Chris Blanchett.

JS2013.527.1550

Charles Francis Annesley Voysey was a
great hero of the period.

JS2013.527.1583

What a superb kaleidoscopic treat. By
refining your focus around the picture a
myriad of gothic forms can be created to
delight the eyes. I don't know the designer
but could we call him 'the master of the
anthemion'?

JS2013.527.1503

Removed from Wemyss Castle in
Fife, c.1985. These are in my Top Five
encaustics. They are robust and intricate,
and never boring to the eye.

JS2013.527.1587

Designed by E.W. Pugin and resplendent in a vast panoply of Christian symbolism. Note the dice thrown by the soldiers beneath Jesus Christ on the cross.

JS2013.527.1499

The Tree of Life, designed by John Pollard Seddon. I waited 20 years to find six of them and then lost patience. My friend Chris Cox of Craven Dunnill Jackfield Ltd then expertly made me three to match.

Encaustic tile panel, Maw & Co., 27 x 27

JS2013.527.1536

A glorious overall picture. Such a majestic design, it demands 16 to show off its sheer grandeur. It is so hard to find Owen Jones designs I am tempted to ascribe this to him. So it is Owen Jones until someone proves me wrong!

Encaustic tile panel, Maw & Co., 23 x 23

JS2013.527.1496

Encaustic tile panel, Craven Dunnill & Co.,
49 x 6

JS2013.527.1788

Left: Hand-painted hospital tile panel
depicting Mary Had a Little Lamb by
Margaret E. Thompson for Doulton,
c.1900, 50½ x 24

JS2013.527.1789

Hand-painted tile panel for a hospital, Daffy Down Dilly by Margaret E. Thompson for Doulton, 22¼ x 49

JS2013.527.1798

These jolly and colourful images were destined and made for children's wards in hospitals. 'Daffy Down Dilly' probably came from a hospital in the Brighton area. TACS have written a good book on this corner of tile history. I am glad that these were saved from the demolition ball and chain. But, the panels should have been relocated in a new hospital – another example of the lack of concern for our heritage!

Glazed encaustic tile panel, Minton Hollins & Co., 15½ x 15½

JS2013.527.1706

Some of the most technical and beautiful of all Victorian tiles. The colours and shapes move as if by magic and allow your eye to move over the surface – never bored, eternally titillated.

Hand-painted tile panel, William De Morgan, 1872–1881, 35½ x 29

JS2013.527.1765

Idealised Italian landscape with a villa and garden. William De Morgan was ill and recuperating in Italy. Halsey Ricardo helped to run the company and no doubt encouraged William to send suitable images to support the works' production.

Hand-painted tile panel from a butcher's shop, designed by William Wise, Minton & Co., 35½ x 17½

JS2013.527.1791

From a Birmingham butcher's shop. An excellent example by the outstanding illustrator for Minton of animals and human figures. He should have insisted on having his signature on his tiles.

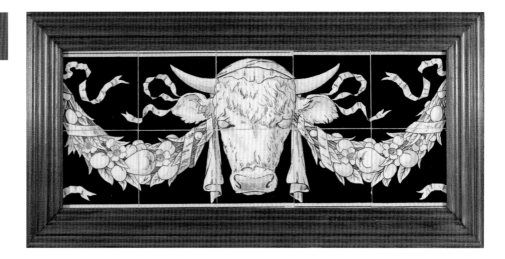

Relief-moulded and coloured glaze tile panel, Carter & Co., c.1905, 20½ x 8¾

JS2013.527.1521

The galleon or Viking sailing vessel was a favourite subject of early 20th-century art. A large house on our road in Prenton, Merseyside, was being demolished so I called my mother to save the huge stained-glass ship window. She came back triumphantly. She had just beaten the ball and chain demolition. It cost her a pound and I love seeing it every day.

Encaustic tile panel, Maw & Co.,
10¼ x 22¼

JS2013.527.1518

Encaustic tile panel, Hargreaves, Craven
Dunnill & Co., 1870, 7½ x 7½

JS2013.527.1624

Relief-moulded tile panel, designed by
George Howard Elphick for the Turkish
baths in north London, also used at
Brighton and elsewhere, Craven Dunnill &
Co., 1902, 18½ x 14¼

JS2013.527.1567

Relief-moulded tile, 'The Pelican in her
Piety', The Campbell Brick & Tile Co.,
c.1880, 13 x 13

JS2013.527.1621

High Christian art with the most
acknowledged example of the animal
kingdom's self-sacrifice. Also part of the
coat of arms of Corpus Christi College,
Oxford.

Hand-painted tile panel, William De
Morgan, 1888–1897, 9½ x 16

JS2013.527.1667

Opposite: Relief-moulded tile, designed by
C.F.A. Voysey, Pilkington tiles, 9 x 15

JS2013.527.1668

I need another leaf to complete the run.

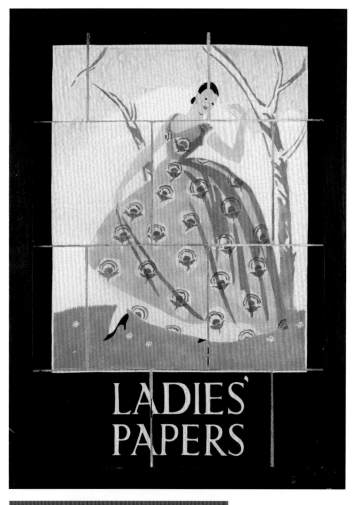

Hand-painted tile panel, designed for W.H. Smith, Carter & Co., c.1930, 17½ x 23¾

JS2013.527.1545

This Poole tile-picture well illustrates one of my themes: the outrageous disposal of our heritage by the senior managers of W.H. Smith & Co. and others. The fine lettering is by Eric Gill. I greatly dislike the loss of so much of our history and so I joined TACS to try to prevent it.

Encaustic tile panel, Minton & Co., 15½ x 21½

JS2013.527.1558

Right: Hand-painted tile panel, designed for W.H. Smith, Carter & Co., c.1930, 20 x 23½

JS2013.527.1586

The writing script is by Eric Gill and the main image is now under the investigation of Dr Ian Betts, the Senior Finds Specialist at the Museum of London. Other Carter tile panels have been discovered at W.H. Smith shops in Bath, Great Malvern, Weston-super-Mare and Torquay.

Encaustic tile panel, W. Godwin, 7⅝ x 31½

JS2013.527.1490

This entrancing run of five tiles in delicious whiplash whirls came from the great tile dealer Matt Townsend. Dresseresque-effect design. In my Top Twenty-five.

Pierced majolica tile made for the Great Stove at the Great Exhibition, designed by A.W.N. Pugin, Minton & Co., 1851, 11½ x 11½

JS2013.527.1652

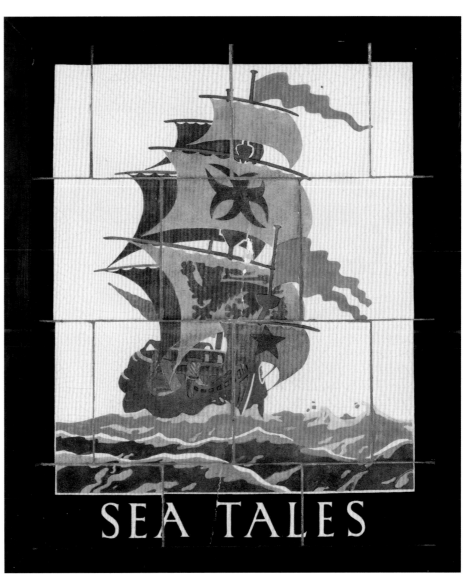

SEA TALES

Hand-painted tile panel, designed for W.H. Smith, Carter & Co., c.1930, 20 x 23¾

JS2013.527.1494

More Poole Pottery tiles c.1920 from a W.H. Smith store. When one thinks of how many W.H. Smith shops existed up to the 50s and 60s, one is aghast at the number of these Poole panels that have been destroyed for development.

Transfer-printed tile panel, designed by
Christopher Dresser, Minton China Works,
1870, 36½ x 12

JS2013.527.1532

Intricate format and stylised floral designs
together with the most intricate yet pleasing
borders. Must be the work of Dresser.

Hand-painted tile, designed by Edward
Bawden, Carter & Co., c.1932, 6½ x 6½

JS2013.527.270

In late 2001 Poole Pottery ran into financial
problems which resulted in its café being
demolished. Along came our knight in
shining armour, Mr Richard Dennis. His
family and friends saved the tiles.

Relief-moulded tile panel, designed by
C.F.A. Voysey, 27½ x 21½

JS2013.527.1535

A cache of these tiles was discovered in
Bristol some thirty years ago. Everyone says
they're by Voysey so you can now 'sell them'
as Voysey … at a Voysey price.

THE JOHN SCOTT TILE COLLECTION

Hand-painted tile, William De Morgan,
6¾ x 6¾

JS2013.527.269

Phantasmagorical ships. William De Morgan
specialised in ships, animals and flowers.
The ships are charmingly eccentric and
highly unlikely to make port! In my Top
Twenty-five.

Hand-painted tiles, designed by Majel
Davidson on H. & R. Johnson blanks,
c.1930, 35¼ x 23

JS2013.527.1572

I bought these and others in a box in
Portobello Market. Said to be designed and
made by Majel Davidson, a member of a
commune of female artists in Scotland.
I don't normally buy figurative art but these
had a singular charm and zest.

Stencil-painted tile from the 'Kitchen'
series, designed by A.B. Read, Carter &
Co., c.1923, 6 x 6

JS2013.527.267

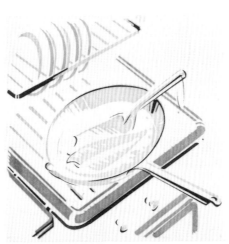

Stencil-painted tile from the 'Kitchen'
series, designed by A.B. Read, Carter &
Co., c.1923, 6 x 6

JS2013.527.268

Stencil-painted tile from the 'Kitchen'
series, designed by A.B. Read, Carter &
Co., c.1923, 6 x 6

JS2013.527.266

Relief-moulded Art Nouveau tile, Henry Richards Tile Co., 6 x 6

JS2013.527.265

Transfer-printed and hand-painted tile, Minton & Co., 1884, 6 x 6

JS2013.527.259

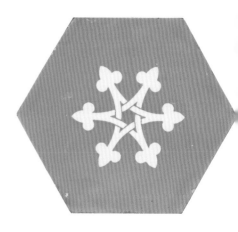

Block-printed and hand-painted tile, Minton & Co., 6½ diameter

JS2013.527.258

Relief-moulded Art Nouveau tile, Lea & Boulton, Tunstall, c.1910, 6½ x 6½

JS2013.527.263

I started collecting Art Nouveau in the early 60s.

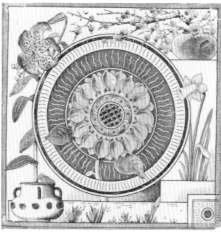

Transfer-printed and hand-tinted tile, 6 x 6

JS2013.527.264

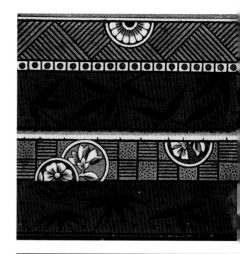

Transfer-printed tile, Malkin Edge & Co., 6 x 6

JS2013.527.260

Right: Glazed encaustic tiles, c.1850, 6 x 6

JS2013.527.261, JS2013.527.262

A nice play on obverse and reverse. Probably Minton but could be from many other good establishments. There did not seem to be stiff penalties for plagiarism!

Relief-moulded tile, Marsden Tile Co.,
6½ x 6½

JS2013.527.256

Transfer-printed tile, Minton China Works,
6 x 6

JS2013.527.257

Very Japanese in style. As I have a wife from that lovely country I do like to be reminded how inspired we were by their decorative art.

Hand screen-printed, tin-glazed tiles from the 'English Countryside' series, designed by Reginald Till, Carter & Co., 1950s, 12 x 12

JS2013.527.253

Carter & Co. always employed top-quality artists and their products are invariably stylish.

Relief-moulded tile, T. & R. Boote,
6½ x 6½

JS2013.527.254

Right: Hand-painted tile from the 'Sporting'
series, designed by Edward Bawden for
Carter & Co. in the 1930s, this is a later
version dated 1964, 7½ x 7

JS2013.527.255

I greatly enjoy Bawden's tiles for their zip
and sardonic humour.

Hand-painted tile, William De Morgan,
6¾ x 6¾

JS2013.527.252

Another crazy galleon. These have been
collectors' items for fifty years or more.

Left: Encaustic tile, W. Godwin, 6 x 6

JS2013.527.1251

Excellent calligraphy. Probably Pugin.

DINING ROOM

Encaustic tile, W. Godwin, c.1860,
6 diameter

JS2013.527.1254

A Godwin circular mat, perhaps for a Pugin
wine decanter, c.1860.

Hand-painted tile, William De Morgan,
1888–1897, 6¾ x 6¾

JS2013.527.1270

Hand-painted tile, William De Morgan,
1888–1897, 7 x 7

JS2013.527.1271

An unstable William De Morgan ship.
They are not fit to float! It's all about being
fabulous!

Hand-painted tile, William De Morgan,
1888–1897, 7½ x 7½

JS2013.527.1276

Hand-painted tile, William De Morgan,
1888–1897, 7 x 7

JS2013.527.1277

Hand-painted tile, Halsey Ricardo design,
William De Morgan, 1888–1897, 11 x 11

JS2013.527.1278

In relief.

Hand-painted tile, William De Morgan,
1882–1888, 9 x 9

JS2013.527.1279

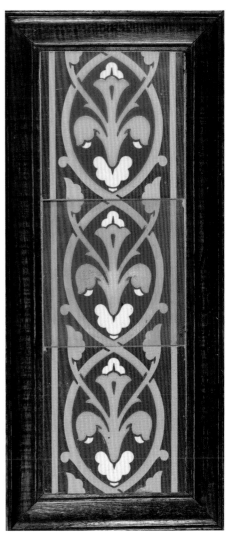

Glazed encaustic tile panels, Maw & Co., 22 x 13

JS2013.527.1752, JS2013.527.1751

An extremely rich dark honey colour glaze gives these tiles a sense of antiquity and grandeur. These had never been laid. A contractor, as today, would tile a building leaving a cache or two of tiles in case they were needed for alterations or repairs.

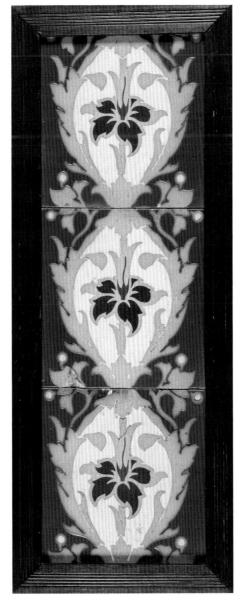

Encaustic tile panel, Maw & Co., 21½ x 9½

JS2013.527.1522

A very strong design by a quality artist.

Right: Encaustic tile panel, Minton & Co., 7½ x 19½

JS2013.527.1515

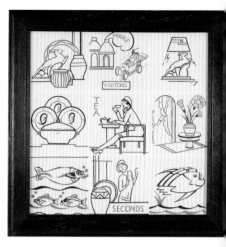

Hand-painted tile panel, designed by Edward Bawden for the Carter & Co. visitors' tea room which was opened in 1932 in Poole, 18 x 18

JS2013.527.1591

These are the tiles saved by Richard Dennis from the 'about to be demolished' Poole Pottery tea room. Very fresh and contemporary.

Encaustic tile panel, Maw & Co., 23 x 11

JS2013.527.1608

A very strong design by a quality artist.

Hand-painted tile, William De Morgan, 6½ x 18½

JS2013.527.1734

Fragment of a fabulous urn. I've had this for 45 years and am still waiting to find the other bits.

Hand-painted tiled tea tray, possibly designed by Sylvia Packard, Packard & Ord Ltd, post-1945, 6½ x 13

JS2013.527.1604

Bought new for mother's birthday in 1953.

Block-printed tile panel, Minton China
Works, 19 x 11

JS2013.527.1607

Perhaps the most beautiful of all the Minton
Victorian tiles – an exquisite blue field with
silver and gold in the form of a stylised
anthemion. How well this has been executed
with such precision and lustre! It has the
same texture as a silver-plated jug or other
shining metal. Now, imagine a room lined
throughout beneath the picture rail with
these tiles. Now light fifty wall brackets with
candles. The effect would be … beyond
words. These great examples encourage
me to assert that this country had, from
1830–1930, the greatest tile production in
the world. Magnificent. Top No. 1 group.

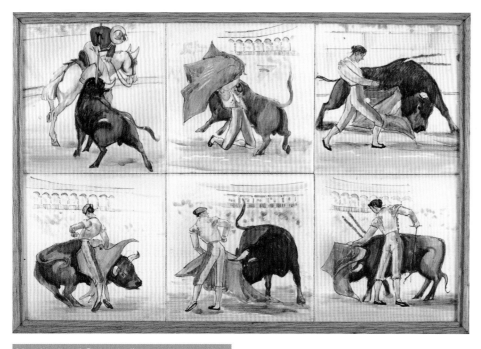

Hand-painted Spanish tile panel, 12½ x 8½

JS2013.527.1670

Hand-painted tile, Caller Herrin design created for MacFisheries by Dora Batty, Carter & Co., 1938–1949, 11¾ x 11¾

JS2013.527.1638

I waited thirty years for this and, even then, broken.

Encaustic tile panel, Minton & Co., 22 x 22

JS2013.527.1585

From the Birch Church, Manchester. My friend Stephen Davis put me on to this and I bought all the floor tiles. Lifting them and getting them down to London was a major job. Probably Pugin. Lovely.

Hand-painted tile panel, designed by William De Morgan, 1882–1888, 23 x 23

JS2013.527.1580

Michael Whiteway found these in a YMCA hostel in north Wales. I waited years for the border tiles which I feel enrich the image as a whole.

JOHN'S OFFICE

From the 'English Countryside' series, designed by Reginald Till, Carter & Co., 1950s, 6 x 6

JS2013.527.530

Encaustic tile, Minton & Co., 6 x 6

JS2013.527.532

This is my favourite encaustic; its black field invites a great design. So simple, so timeless. No. 1.

Encaustic tile, designed by A.W.N. Pugin, Minton & Co., c.1830, 6 x 6

JS2013.527.535

Transfer-printed and hand-coloured landscape from the 'New Domesday Book of Kent' series, designed by Donald Maxwell, Doulton, 5½ x 6½

JS2013.527.534

Relief-moulded tile, designed by Alfred Waterhouse, Minton & Co., 1865, 8 x 8

JS2013.527.543

Illustrated in *Terracotta Designs* by Colin Cunningham. A design by Alfred Waterhouse for the Natural History Museum probably unused.

Encaustic tile, designed by John Pollard Seddon, Maw & Co., 6 x 6

JS2013.527.533

Screen-printed tile, designed by Ann Clark
on an H. & R. Johnson blank, 1975, 6 x 6

JS2013.527.531

Gorgeous – Number One in my
contemporary list. Ann Clark has the highest
spiritual 'touch' for tile design. A genius.

Encaustic tile, Boch Frères Maubeuge, Belgium, c.1880, 6 x 6

JS2013.527.536

A leaping hound encircled by Gothic foliage. I dream and hope it is by Viollet-le-Duc.

Transfer-printed tile, The Campbell Brick & Tile Co., 1875–1882, 6 x 6

JS2013.527.537

Compellingly attractive.

Hand-painted tile, William De Morgan, 6¾ x 6¾

JS2013.527.538

With De Morgan it's either ships, flowers or animals – no human figures.

Hand-painted tile by Majel Davidson on a J.C. Edwards (Ruabon) blank, 1930s, 6 x 6

JS2013.527.539

These figures have a most attractive vivacity.

Encaustic tile, Minton & Co., 1870s, 5⅞ x 5⅞

JS2013.527.540

In my Top Ten. The faces may be the Devil or a Green Man. An excellent design – a black field is always a good start.

Transfer-printed classical scene designed by John Moyr Smith, Minton China Works, 8 x 8

JS2013.527.541

The hostess sits in a beautifully designed aesthetic chair, with aesthetic vases.

Left: Relief-moulded majolica tile, Minton Hollins, 8 x 8

JS2013.527.542

Exquisite, also in my Top Ten. I cannot pin down the designer, Dresser? Owen Jones?

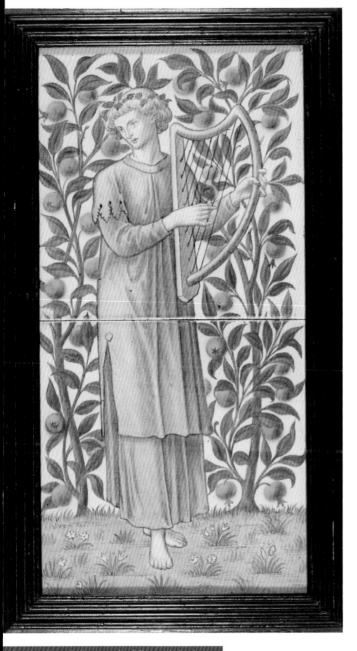

Hand-painted tile panels, Minstrel design
by William Morris, 1870s, 7½ x 13½

JS2013.527.1468, JS2013.527.1471

Encaustic tile, Minton & Co., 3 x 3

JS2013.527.1469

Encaustic tile, Minton & Co., 3 x 3

JS2013.527.1470

Hand-painted tile, 6½ x 6½

JS2013.527.1472

Just a great little design.

Hand-painted tile, William De Morgan, 1888–1897, 6¾ x 6¾

JS2013.527.1473

The ship is set to sail backwards! Replete with quixotic charm.

Hand-painted tile, William De Morgan, 1888–1897, 6¾ x 6¾

JS2013.527.1474

Hand-painted tile, William De Morgan, 1888–1897, 7½ x 7½

JS2013.527.1475

Crazy ship.

Left: Hand-painted tile, William De Morgan, 1882–1888, 7½ x 7½

JS2013.527.1476

Hand-painted tile, William De Morgan, 1888–1897, 7½ x 7½

JS2013.527.1478

The most top heavy ship ever!

Relief-moulded tile, Copeland, 8¼ x 8¼

JS2013.527.1479

Very rich polychrome and delightful toning. Despite chips and scouring, I love this.

Hand-painted tile, William De Morgan, 1888–1897, 7¾ x 7¾

JS2013.527.1480

Crazy ship.

Hand-painted tile, Packard & Ord, 5¾ x 5¾

JS2013.527.1482

A present from Michael Manser of Lincoln College, Oxford. We went on a Spanish rugby tour together. The Polly Tea Rooms in Marlborough served the most delicious homemade cakes but, for me, the main attraction was the encaustic tiles on the gingham tablecloths, used as teapot stands.

Photographic tile, 8 x 7

JS2013.527.1481

Raised line moulded tile, Minton Hollins & Co., 8 x 8

JS2013.527.1477

A flamboyant jewel of a tile with a floreated oriental feel.

TAKKO'S OFFICE

Hand-painted tile from the 'Nursery Toys' series, designed by Dora Batty for Carter & Co., 1930s, 6 x 6

JS2013.527.711

Right: Transfer-printed tile, Wedgwood, c.1880, 6 x 6

JS2013.527.712

Relief-moulded tile, a design based on Moorish plasterwork at the Alhambra Palace, Maw & Co., 6 x 6

JS2013.527.709

Islamic design. I need another three to complete the picture.

Transfer-printed and hand-painted tile, Minton China Works, 6 x 6

JS2013.527.710

Has to be Dresser – so intricately designed.

Relief-moulded majolica tile, Minton & Co., 6¾ x 6¾

JS2013.527.705

Relief-moulded majolica tile, Minton & Co., 7 x 7

JS2013.527.706

With its sparkling polychrome majolica finish, this is in my Top Ten. A glorious delectable object that was a pleasure to have on my desk.

Encaustic tile, W. Godwin, 4¼ x 4¼

JS2013.527.707

Probably A.W.N. Pugin.

Encaustic tile, The Campbell Brick & Tile Co., 6 x 4

JS2013.527.708

My collection should have been more selective. Lots that I have bought were interesting but took up space and irritated my wife. So I put up a narrow shelf above the picture rail.

Encaustic tile, Minton & Co., c.1840, 5⅛ x 5⅛

JS2013.527.713

Hand-painted tile, Columbine design by William Morris, 1860s, 6 x 6

JS2013.527.714

Transfer-printed tile, designed by
Christopher Dresser, Minton China Works,
c.1875, 8 x 8

JS2013.527.715

This is in my Top Ten.

Block-printed and painted tile, designed by
A.W.N. Pugin, Minton China Works, 8 x 8

JS2013.527.716

Relief-moulded tile, Minton Hollins & Co.,
6 x 6

JS2013.527.717

Relief-moulded border tiles, Minton & Co.,
7½ x 7½

JS2013.527.719, JS2013.527.720

Transfer-printed tile, Minton, 8 x 7

JS2013.527.718

Transfer-printed tiles, 6 x 6

JS2013.527.722, JS2013.527.721

Lustre tile, designed by Lewis F. Day, Maw
& Co., 6 x 6

JS2013.527.728

I always considered Lewis F. Day inferior to
De Morgan but this was one of his winners.
Excellent.

View of Stokesay Castle in Shropshire, designed by George H. Grundy for The Photo Decorated Tile Co. on a Pilkington blank, c.1900. 6 x 6

JS2013.527.724

Left: Transfer-printed tile, designed by Owen Gibbons, Maw & Co., 6 x 6

JS2013.527.723

Line-impressed tile, line-filled with contrasting colour, Maw & Co., 6 x 6

JS2013.527.725

Transfer-printed tile, designed by A.W.N. Pugin, Minton Hollins & Co., 6 x 6

JS2013.527.726

Block-printed tile, Minton Hollins & Co., 6 x 6

JS2013.527.727

Relief-moulded tile, designed by
C.F.A. Voysey for Pilkington's Tile & Pottery
Co. Ltd, c.1905, 6 x 6

JS2013.527.730

Lovely crisp design and execution.

Relief-moulded tile, designed by
C.F.A. Voysey, Pilkington's Tile & Pottery
Co. Ltd, c.1910, 6 x 6

JS2013.527.733

A beautifully styled ship.

Tube-lined tile, Pilkington, c.1910, 6 x 6

JS2013.527.729

Transfer-printed tile from the 'Farm' series,
designed by William Wise, Minton China
Works, 6 x 6

JS2013.527.731

Glazed encaustic tile panel, W. Godwin,
12 x 12

JS2013.527.1731

From the 'Coloured Dutch' series,
designed by Joseph Roelants, Carter &
Co., c.1930s, 6 x 6

JS2013.527.732

Tube-lined tile, possibly after a design by
Charlotte Rhead, H. & R. Johnson, 1927,
8 x 4

JS2013.527.734

Tube-lined tile, possibly after a design by
Charlotte Rhead, H. & R. Johnson, 1927,
8 x 4

JS2013.527.735

Hand-painted tile panel, designed by
William James Neatby, Doulton, 25½ x 12¾

JS2013.527.1732

These are the three Kings that came to
Jesus bearing gifts. The best example of his
work is in Harrods Food Hall – a sumptuous
display.

Relief-moulded tile panel, Maw & Co.,
37½ x 11

JS2013.527.1714

Exquisitely luxurious with a huge range of
colours. Luckily I had an oak frame to fit so
it's a superb ensemble. In my Top Three.

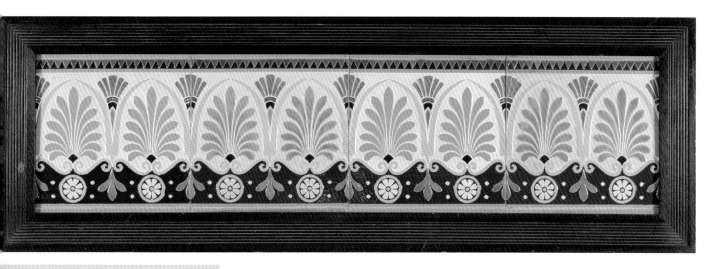

Relief-moulded tile panel, Minton Hollins & Co., 35½ x 11½

JS2013.527.1795

These are universally superb. In my Top Five.

Relief-moulded tile panel, Minton Hollins & Co., 9 x 31¾

JS2013.527.1611

These tiles are my Top Ten favourites.

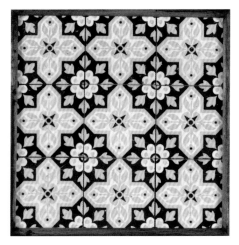

Encaustic tile panel, W. Godwin, 13 x 13

JS2013.527.1747

Encaustic tile panel, Minton & Co., 16¼ x 16¼

JS2013.527.1528

Sometimes if I am missing one to make up a set of four, I find a fourth of the same design but in a different colourway. I use the odd one; it certainly irritates my eye considerably less than a bare gap.

Hand-painted stencilled tile panel, designed by Polly Brace for Dunsmore Tiles, c.1928, 20½ x 26½

JS2013.527.1739

Collecting is a bit like hunting. The caveman had to make a kill for his family to eat. On Saturday I like to find something in Portobello Market, bring it home, clean off its cement and put it in the rack. Then I know I'm alive!

Encaustic tile panel, W. Godwin, 15¼ x 15¼

JS2013.527.1526

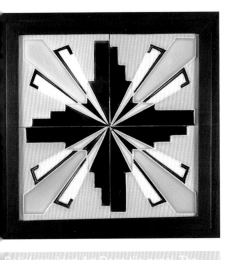

Relief-moulded Art Deco tile panel, The
Campbell Brick & Tile Co., 1957, originally
produced by Maw & Co. in the 1920s,
14½ x 14½
JS2013.527.1622

Hand-painted tile panel, Daisy design by
William Morris, 1860s, 9 x 15
JS2013.527.1605

Relief-moulded tile panel, designed by
Edmund Kent, Pilkington's Tile & Pottery
Co. Ltd, 1983, 16 x 11
JS2013.527.1606

Hand-painted tile panel, William De
Morgan, 1888–1897, 15 x 15
JS2013.527.1600

Relief-moulded majolica tile panel, Maw &
Co., 15 x 15
JS2013.527.1596

Pierced majolica tiles made for the Great Stove at the Great Exhibition, designed by A.W.N. Pugin, Minton & Co., 1851, 20½ x 20½

JS2013.527.1575

Can't be sure these are originals from the Stove! This set has been lent to at least ten major exhibitions around the world. Many of the tiles had holes for the hot air to warm the rooms. These huge stoves were much used for heating palaces in Europe.

Relief-moulded tile panel, Minton Hollins & Co., 25½ x 9½

JS2013.527.1563

Relief-moulded portrait tiles, Minton Hollins & Co., 25 x 9½

JS2013.527.1726

Below: Hand-painted Sinbad and his crew firing arrows at the giant Roc, William De Morgan, 1882–1888, 26 x 10

JS2013.527.1684

Encaustic tile panel, Minton & Co., c.1840, 20½ x 20½

JS2013.527.1544

Well distressed with a honey glaze for a medieval effect.

Right: Encaustic tile panel, Minton & Co., c.1850, 17¾ x 17¾

JS2013.527.1578

Encaustic tile panel, Chamberlain & Co., 20 x 20

JS2013.527.1504

Hand-painted tile panel, William De Morgan, 1888–1897, 15½ x 23¼

JS2013.527.1495

JS2013.527.1573

JS2013.527.1679

The Carter artists had a peculiar penchant
for design on a 6 x 6 space! I particularly
praise Leslie Elsden, Dora Batty, Edward
Bawden, Harold Stabler, Reginald Till and
E.E. Stickland.

Encaustic tiles relating to John Talbot,
16th Earl of Shrewsbury, designed by
A.W.N. Pugin, Minton & Co., 23 x 11½

JS2013.527.1768

Talbot was Pugin's chief patron and this
partnership saw the completion of many
outstanding Gothic buildings in Pugin's
short life. His favourite was St Giles at
Cheadle. Go and see it. A sacred home of
the master's finest work. In my Top Eight.

Relief-moulded tile panel, Minton Hollins & Co., 18 x 18

JS2013.527.1507

n the Indo-Islamic style, a fascinating
olend of two of the great art traditions.
May I refer readers to Edgar Allan Poe's
unacknowledged masterpiece, *The Domain
of Arnheim*? The admixture of styles created
his celestial city.

Transfer-printed and hand-coloured tile,
designed by A.W.N. Pugin, Minton
& Co., 14½ x 14½

JS2013.527.1623

Designed by Thea Bridges, Packard &
Ord, c.1950, 13 x 13

JS2013.527.1755

Encaustic tile panel, W. Godwin, 9½ x 9½

JS2013.527.1676

Beautifully and impeccably made. A jewel-
ike effect with the varied and sharp colours
of the different clays.

Encaustic tile panel, W. Godwin, 9 x 9

JS2013.527.1666

Encaustic tile, designed by A.W.N. Pugin
for the Palace of Westminster, Minton &
Co., 13 x 13

JS2013.527.1620

Perhaps a discard from the Palace store
room. Some items do slip out!

Relief-moulded tile panel, designed by
C.F.A. Voysey, Pilkington, 21 x 11½

JS2013.527.1610

Possibly from a swimming pool? I found the
border tiles separately – they set off good
tiles quite dramatically. A nice tinge of the
oriental. In my Top Ten.

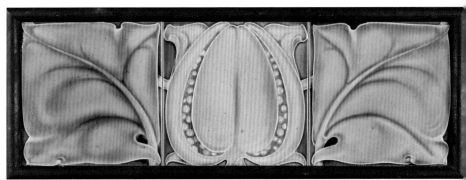

Tube-lined Art Nouveau tile panel, Marsden
Tile Co., 7 x 19

JS2013.527.1525

Lustrous and beautiful. Probably Voysey.

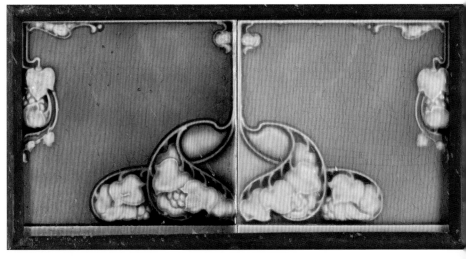

Relief-moulded Art Nouveau tile panel,
6½ x 13

JS2013.527.1603

Probably Voysey.

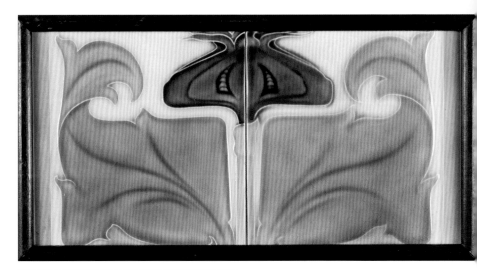

Relief-moulded Art Nouveau tile panel,
6½ x 13

JS2013.527.1601

Probably Voysey.

Encaustic tile panel, Maw & Co., 9 x 9

JS2013.527.1665

Transfer-printed tile panel, designed by Christopher Dresser, Minton China Works, 11¾ x 21½

JS2013.527.1565

Designed by my hero Dr Christopher Dresser.

Hand-painted tile panel, William De Morgan, 1888–1897, 25 x 8¾

JS2013.527.1566

Printed outline and hand-coloured mosaic-style tile, Copeland, 9¾ x 9¾

JS2013.527.1660

Inspired by excavations in Pompeii, Herculaneum or London.

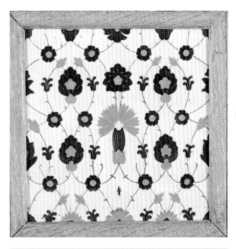

Relief-moulded tile, Minton Hollins & Co., 9 x 9

JS2013.527.1661

Transfer-printed tile depicting Poole Quay designed by Bernard Charles, Carter & Co., 1960s, 11 x 11

JS2013.527.1663

Left: Printed outline and hand-coloured mosaic-style tile, Copeland, 10 x 10

JS2013.527.1662

This type of tile was no doubt created following the excavations at Pompeii; the design was possibly copied from the original mosaic pavements found there.

Photographic tile, The Photo Decorated Tile Co., c.1900, 9½ x 9½

JS2013.527.1634

A delightful image to enrich your Welsh dresser.

Screen-printed tile, designed by Joseph Roelants, Carter & Co., 1951, 11¼ x 11¼

JS2013.527.1640

Block-printed and hand-coloured tile, designed by A.W.N. Pugin, Minton & Co., 11¾ x 11¾

JS2013.527.1644

An outstanding design in great demand well after Pugin's death in 1852.

Opus Sectile, Powells of Whitefriars, 10¾ x 10¾

JS2013.527.1642

Transfer-printed and hand-coloured mosaic-style tile, Copeland, 11½ x 11½

JS2013.527.1643

Transfer-printed and hand-coloured tile, Copeland, 9 x 9

JS2013.527.1648

Teapot stand, Minton & Co., 6 x 6

JS2013.527.1653

Photographic tile showing Windsor Castle by George Grundy for The Photo Decorated Tile Co. on a Pilkington blank, c.1900, 8½ x 8½

JS2013.527.1656

Hand-painted tile, William De Morgan, 1888–1897, 9 x 9

JS2013.527.1657

Right: Relief-moulded promotional paperweight, Minton Hollins & Co., 4 x 3

JS2013.527.903

287

Encaustic tile, Minton & Co., 1868,
10 diameter

JS2013.527.1655

Another favourite. I saw the same image in a
floor at Osborne House, Isle of Wight.
I wonder if this is Queen Victoria herself or
one of her daughters.

Hand-painted tile panel, William De Morgan, 15½ x 33½

JS2013.527.1782

This is a glorious vertical. The repeat uses six tiles but the pattern is so intricate as to profit from more. Curvilinear and exotic. I waited 15 years to get these.

Italian hand-painted tile, c.1880, 20 x 25¾

JS2013.527.1577

Encaustic tile, Minton & Co., 1864, 6½ diameter

JS2013.527.904

Very skilful blending of black and grey. Happy reflections of my favourite wireless *cloisonné* Japanese vase.

Transfer-printed and hand-coloured mosaic-style teapot stand, Copeland, 10 x 10

JS2013.527.1658

The mosaic is a sepia design of a Roman pavement revealed after a famous excavation of London Wall in the City of London.

Encaustic tile, W. Godwin, 6 x 6

JS2013.527.905

Transfer-printed tile, Maw & Co., 6 x 6

JS2013.527.906

Encaustic tile, The Campbell Brick & Tile Co., 6 x 6

JS2013.527.907

From Wemyss Castle in Scotland.

Encaustic tile, Minton & Co., 1858, 6 x 6

JS2013.527.908

Pugin, probably E.W.

Encaustic tile by Chris Cox after A.W.N. Pugin, from the Palace of Westminster Project, Craven Dunnill Jackfield Ltd, 2009, 6 x 6

JS2013.527.909

Relief-moulded tile, designed by Harold
Stabler for the London Underground,
Carter & Co., 1930s, 6 x 6

JS2013.527.911

Very keen indeed on these lovely tiles
made under the masterly touch, style and
panache of Frank Pick. He made the London
Underground a symbol of modern Britain.
The tiles, designed by Stabler, were used in
many of the stations and illustrated London
landmark buildings and emblems. It is a
crying shame that most have been removed.

Hand-painted tile, designed by Alistair Macduff for Dorincourt Industries, 1955, 6 x 6

JS2013.527.913

Encaustic border tile, Minton & Co., 1858, 6 x 6

JS2013.527.912

I always feel Edward Pugin was a step behind his father Augustus in most of his works. However, the calligraphy of this tile by Edward Pugin is quite unsurpassed in its blending of gothic forms and nature. It came from the Grange in Ramsgate and was given to me and my wife Takko by Dom Bede Millard 'in token of friendship and esteem'. I find the typography of this image of outstanding merit.

Right: Screen-printed fireplace tile, The Campbell Brick & Tile Co., 6 x 6

JS2013.527.914

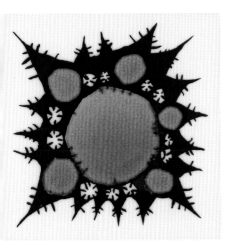

Hand screen-printed wax resist tile, designed by Ann Clark, Kenneth Clark Ceramics on an H. & R. Johnson blank, 1972, 6 x 6

JS2013.527.915

Hand screen-printed wax resist tile, designed by Ann Clark, Kenneth Clark Ceramics on an H. & R. Johnson blank, 1972, 6 x 6

JS2013.527.916

Hand screen-printed wax resist tile, designed by Ann Clark, Kenneth Clark Ceramics on an H. & R. Johnson blank, 1960, 6 x 6

JS2013.527.917

Relief-moulded tile, designed by C.F.A. Voysey as a self-portrait depicting the devil, J.C. Edwards (Ruabon), c.1900, 6 x 6

JS2013.527.910

Fans of Voysey should view his portrait at the Art Workers' Guild in London. A most august and severe visage gazes on the visitor. It looks so at odds with our greatest domestic architect of the early 20th century, and designer of such charming and homely furniture and metalwork.

Hand-painted tile, possibly designed by Alistair Macduff, Dorincourt Industries on a Carter & Co. blank, 1960, 6 x 6

JS2013.527.918

Hand screen-printed wax resist tile, Father Christmas design by Ann Clark, Kenneth Clark Ceramics on an H. & R. Johnson blank, 1959, 6 x 6

JS2013.527.919

Most captivating. Ann is a 'Picasso' of the contemporary tile world. Top No. 1 pile!

Hand screen-printed tile from the 'English Countryside' series, designed by Reginald Till, Carter & Co., 1953, 6 x 6

JS2013.527.920

Hand-painted tile from the 'Nursery Toys' series, designed by Dora Batty, Carter & Co., 1930s, 6 x 6

JS2013.527.921

Stencilled and hand-painted tile, Caller Herrin design created for MacFisheries by Dora Batty, Carter & Co., 1938–1946, 6 x 6

JS2013.527.922

I much admire the extended image crossing the line of a tile border. This lifts the subject and highlights it.

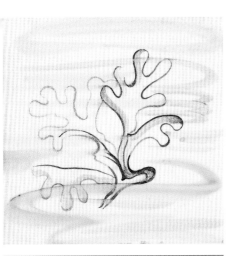

Hand-painted tile from the 'Sea Plants' series, designed by Phillis Butler, Carter & Co., 1960s, 6 x 6

JS2013.527.923

Hand-painted tile from the 'Toy Box' series, designed by Dora Batty, Carter & Co., c.1930, 6 x 6

JS2013.527.924

Hand-painted tile from the 'Nursery Toys' series, designed by Dora Batty, Carter & Co., c.1930, 6 x 6

JS2013.527.925

Left: Stencilled and hand-painted tiles from the 'Farm' series, designed by E.E. Stickland, Carter & Co., 1950s, 2 x 6

JS2013.527.926

Makes a charming wicker work tray.

Designed by Jun Takegoshi, 9¾ x 9¾

JS2013.527.1232

A Japanese artist that we befriended in Japan. We introduced him to the Fine Art Society where he had great success. This tile is heavily inspired by Islamic art which Jun greatly admires.

Right: Designed by Jun Takegoshi, 9¼ x 9¼

JS2013.527.1233

Designed and made by Jun Takegoshi.

Relief-moulded tile, designed by C.F.A. Voysey, Medmenham Pottery, Marlow, c.1904, 7¾ x 7¾

JS2013.527.1234

Relief-moulded photographic tile, designed by George Cartlidge, Sherwin and Cotton, c.1900, 7½ x 7½

JS2013.527.1235

Hand-painted stoneware tile with Weeping Willow design by Bernard Leach, St Ives Pottery, Cornwall, c.1930, 6$\frac{7}{10}$ x 6$\frac{7}{10}$

JS2013.527.1248

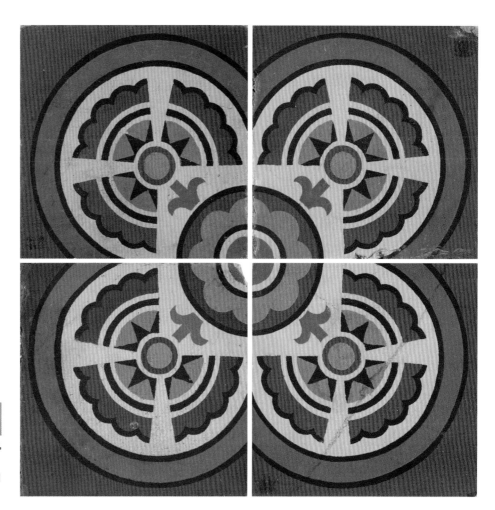

Right: Encaustic tiles, Boch Frères
Maubeuge, Belgium, c.1880, 6⁸/₁₀ x 6⁸/₁₀

JS2013.527.1240, JS2013.527.1242, JS2013.527.1239,
JS2013.527.1241

Good design, but the execution and material
are different to Minton etc.

Left: Encaustic tiles, Boch Frères
Maubeuge, Belgium, c.1880, 6½ x 6½

JS2013.527.1243, JS2013.527.1236, JS2013.527.1244,
JS2013.527.1245

Encaustic tile, Minton & Co., 6¾ x 6¾

JS2013.527.1257

Encaustic tiles, Boch Frères Maubeuge, Belgium, c.1880, 6⁸⁄₁₀ x 6⁸⁄₁₀

JS2013.527.1247, JS2013.527.1246, JS2013.527.1238, JS2013.527.1237

On a Harlequins rugby tour I saw a magnificent set of these encaustics by Villeroy & Boch in L'Hotel du Gare, Main Square, St Jean de Luz.

Relief-moulded majolica tile, possibly designed by E.W. Pugin, Minton & Co., 13 x 13

JS2013.527.1729

A beautiful product like this will stand the test of hundreds of years.

Left: Encaustic tiles, Boch Frères Maubeuge, Belgium, c.1880, 6⁷⁄₁₀ x 6⁷⁄₁₀

JS2013.527.1250, JS2013.527.1249

Very decorative but not a patch on English encaustics for richness of colour and sharpness of glaze.

GARDEN ROOM

Left: Silk-screen printed tile panel, designed by John Piper depicting the four seasons, Fulham Pottery, 1983, 18 x 18

JS2013.527.1514

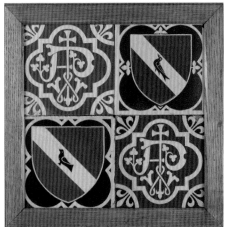

Encaustic tile panel, designed by A.W.N. Pugin, Minton & Co., 14 x 14

JS2013.527.1564

Coat of arms of W.W.N. Pugin from his home The Grange, Ramsgate. The martlet is frequently depicted without legs – like Pugin himself … always 'on the go'. En Avant – family motto.

Encaustic tile panel relating to John Talbot, 16th Earl of Shrewsbury, designed by A.W.N. Pugin, Minton & Co., 15 x 20

JS2013.527.1594

BATHROOMS

Block-printed and hand-coloured tile, designed by A.W.N. Pugin, Minton China Works, 11 x 11

JS2013.527.284

Block-printed and hand-coloured tile, Minton Hollins & Co., 6¾ x 6¾

JS2013.527.288

Transfer-printed and hand-painted tile, designed by A.W.N. Pugin, Minton & Co., 7½ x 7½

JS2013.527.287

Hand-painted tile, William De Morgan, 1888–1897, 14 x 8

JS2013.527.285

De Morgan, like Maws' Victorian artists, drew inspiration from the ancient world. So, here is a view of a Henley Regatta in Naples Bay!

Glazed encaustic tile, c.1845, 7 x 7

JS2013.527.292

Below: Hand-painted stencilled tile panel, designed by Polly Brace for Dunsmore Tiles, c.1928, 4½ x 12½

JS2013.527.286

Tube-lined tile, Carter & Co., 1951, 6 x 6 within 7½ x 7½

JS2013.527.290

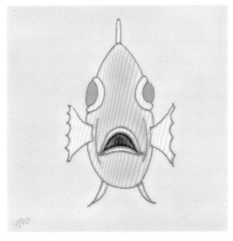

Tube-lined tile, Carter & Co., post-war design on a 1939 blank, 6 x 6

JS2013.527.291

Tube-lined tile, Carter & Co., post-war design on a 1940 blank, 6 x 6

JS2013.527.289

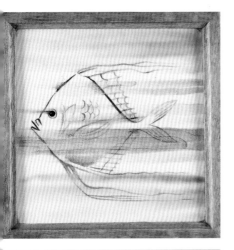

Hand-painted tile, designed by Polly Brace for Dunsmore Tiles, c.1930, 6½ x 6½

JS2013.527.293

Hand-painted tile, designed by Polly Brace for Dunsmore Tiles on a Minton blank, c.1932, 4 x 4

JS2013.527.294

Hand-painted tile, designed by Polly Brace for Dunsmore Tiles on a Minton blank, c.1932, 4 x 4

JS2013.527.295

Hand-painted tile, designed by Polly Brace for Dunsmore Tiles on a Minton blank, c.1932, 6 x 6

JS2013.527.316

Encaustic tile, W. Godwin, 6 x 6

JS2013.527.296

Encaustic tile, W. Godwin, 6 x 6

JS2013.527.297

Block-printed tile, designed by A.W.N. Pugin, Minton Hollins & Co., 6¾ x 6¾

JS2013.527.298

Relief-moulded tile, Minton Hollins & Co., 8 x 8

JS2013.527.504

Very modern in aspect but sophisticated and appealing – some master designed this.

Transfer-printed and hand-painted tile, Moorish design that was originally in plasterwork, Minton China Works, 8 x 8

JS2013.527.500

Islamic inspiration. Desperate for another three – or 15!

Moorish geometric design, Minton & Co., 8 x 8

JS2013.527.505

A fine design.

Transfer-printed and hand-painted tiles,
possibly designed by Owen Jones, 8 x 8

JS2013.527.507, JS2013.527.506, JS2013.527.508

Block-printed and hand-painted tiles, Minton
Hollins & Co., 1875–1910, 8 x 8

JS2013.527.501, JS2013.527.502, JS2013.527.503

Hand-painted tile, William De Morgan,
1888–1897, 53½ x 11. Two of these tiles
are reproductions made for John Scott in
2001 to complete the panel.

JS2013.527.1780

Fabulous panel. Used on the summer house
at the rear of 8 Addison Road, London
W14. Designed by De Morgan's partner
Halsey Ricardo.

Relief-moulded tiles, Craven Dunnill & Co., 9½ x 12

JS2013.527.496, JS2013.527.495

I feel I have seen these in the Brighton Museum. I am sure they are very important and I should have bought more. But there is the question of space!

Below: Relief-moulded tiles, Minton Hollins & Co., 8 x 8

JS2013.527.499, JS2013.527.497, JS2013.527.498

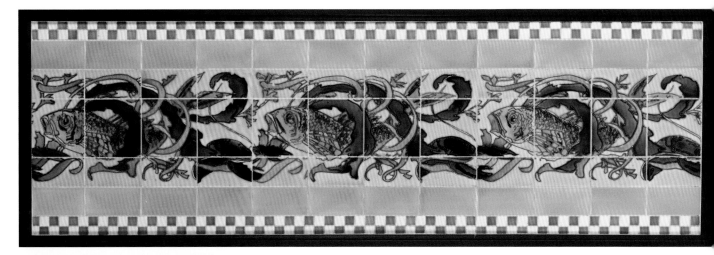

Tube-lined tile panel, Pilkington, 1920–1930, 74½ x 25

JS2013.527.1792

A magnificent panel. Bought from Michael Whiteway from a very fine 1920s mansion in Hertfordshire. One can never get details of provenance which is utterly infuriating and historically disastrous.

Hand-painted tile panel, William De
Morgan, 18¼ x 10

JS2013.527.1519

In my Top Twenty! A rich mélange of
serpent and floral whirls influenced by
William Morris.

Hand-painted tiles from the 'Nursery Toys'
series, designed by Dora Batty, Carter &
Co., 1930s, 37 x 25

JS2013.527.1784

Right: Stencilled and hand-painted tile
panel, 19 x 19

JS2013.527.1510

Hand-painted tile panel, decorated by talented amateur on Minton blanks, Minton & Co., 17¾ x 9¾

JS2013.527.1517

In my Top Five. Exquisitely painted by a Japanese hand. The Minton moulded sign on the back has been crudely erased. Why? The scene itself – a simple country picture of two birds and an insect set before a sky full of birds and Mount Fuji.

Hand-painted stencilled tiles, designed by Polly Brace for Dunsmore Tiles, 1930s, 15 x 15

JS2013.527.1616

Charming for a children's nursery.

Hand-painted tile panel, William De Morgan, 1888–1897, 16½ x 8¾

JS2013.527.1516

In my Top Twenty. A wondrous sinuosity of crane, river and fish.

Hand-painted tile panel from the 'Sporting' series, designed by Edward Bawden for Carter & Co., 1920–1950, 12¾ x 12¾

JS2013.527.1711

Encaustic tile panel, W. Godwin, 13 x 13

JS2013.527.1718

Encaustic tile panel, W. Godwin, 13½ x 13½

JS2013.527.1712

Good but no patch on his 'Class in Sport' (a title I invented). There's Lady Fotheringday Hepplethwaite-Claughtonbuck in her silk shirt and posh hat calling in the hounds and there's Fred casting his plug for pike – 'Coarse Fishing' – in his grandfather's old slouch hat. A lovely joke! No one touched the class divide with such poignancy as Bawden.

Hand-painted tile panel, William De Morgan, 1882–1888, 17¾ x 11½

JS2013.527.1561

Stencilled tile panel from the 'Kitchen' series, designed by Alfred Read for Carter & Co., 1950s, 12½ x 12½

JS2013.527.1675

Right: Hand-painted tile panel, William De Morgan, 1888–1897, 15½ x 25½

JS2013.527.1489

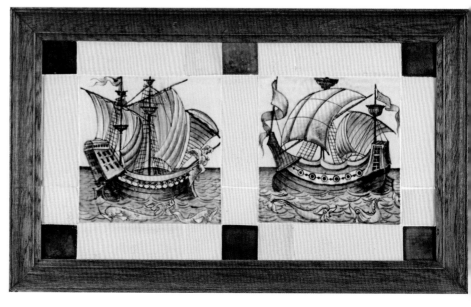

Hand-painted tiles from the 'Play Box' series, designed by Alfred Read for Carter & Co., 1950s version, 27¼ x 21½

JS2013.527.1533

Encaustic tile panel, designed by A.W.N. Pugin, Minton & Co., 8½ x 8½

JS2013.527.1646

I always find a dark field emphasises the decoration and this is no exception. Here is part of the Pugin family crest. The Martlet, always on the wing, is often portrayed by Pugin without feet. Thus does he present himself as tirelessly striving to complete his multitudinous tasks.

Encaustic tile panel, Minton & Co., 20¼ x 20¼

JS2013.527.1582

I removed these from the Birch Church, Manchester. The owner was making something else out of the church so I had a free rein but limited time. The tiles are mighty heavy; such was the weight in my little Volkswagen Scirocco that the back tyre blew out!

Hand-painted tiles, designed by Polly Brace for Dunsmore Tiles, c.1935, 20½ x 20½

JS2013.527.1541

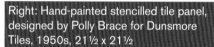

Right: Hand-painted stencilled tile panel, designed by Polly Brace for Dunsmore Tiles, 1950s, 21½ x 21½

JS2013.527.1534

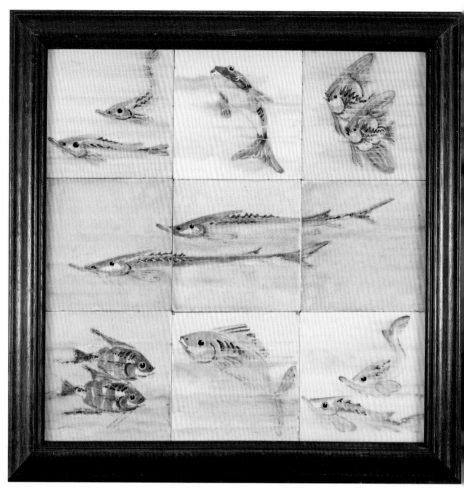

Left: Tile panel, designed by Lewis F. Day, 20 x 20

JS2013.527.1539

Opposite: Hand-painted tile panel, William De Morgan, 31½ x 22½

JS2013.527.1571

Top Four tile, with a monkey at the helm – real De Morgan madness! Fabulous.

Encaustic tile panel, possibly designed by John Pollard Seddon, 55 x 7

JS2013.527.1781

The twirly whirlies. They form part of an exotic, stylised floral frieze. An excellent design. Again, much enhanced having a dark field. Top Six. Entrancing.

Encaustic tile, W. Godwin, 6 x 6

JS2013.527.1252

Transfer-printed tile, Minton China Works, 6 x 6

JS2013.527.1253

Encaustic tile, Minton & Co., 6 x 6

JS2013.527.1256

Right: Encaustic tile panel, Maw & Co., 28½ x 28½

JS2013.527.1531

I greatly admire this pattern by Bruce J. Talbert, one of the most prolific designers of the Gothic Revival age.

JS2013.527.1786

From the Birch Church, Manchester. A
magnificent panel almost certainly designed
by A.W.N. Pugin for Minton. It exemplifies
the importance of gathering together
enough tiles to make a complete picture.

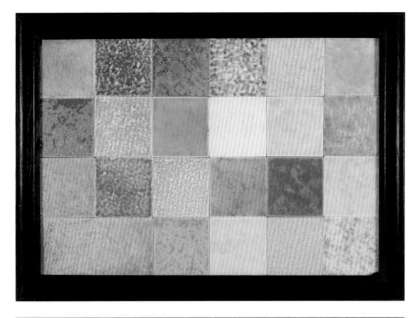

Glazed sample tiles from Pilkington, 17 x 23, 19 x 27, 20¾ x 17¾, 22½ x 18

JS2013.527.1511, JS2013.527.1513, JS2013.527.1557, JS2013.527.1497

I bought all these tiles at Christie's, South Kensington. I am certain they were trials for various glaze finishes. They are superb tiles from the Pilkington factory with a gorgeous range of colours, surfaces and lustres.

BEDROOMS

Encaustic tile, c.1884, 6 x 6

JS2013.527.278

Very attractive because of faults! The air had not been beaten out of the clay in the blunger so it exploded and broke a hole in the surface.

Encaustic tile, W. Godwin, 4 x 4

JS2013.527.272

Encaustic tile, Minton & Co., c.1840, 6 x 6

JS2013.527.277

From St Mary's Convent in Hunter's Road, Birmingham, a wondrous treasure trove of A.W.N. Pugin.

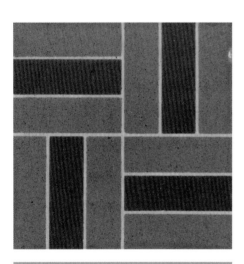

Glazed tile, W. Godwin, 6 x 6

JS2013.527.271

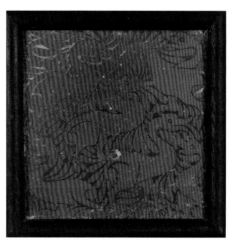

Hand-painted tile, William De Morgan, 7¼ x 7¼

JS2013.527.279

Encaustic tile, Minton & Co., 1860, 6¾ x 6¾

JS2013.527.280

Encaustic tile, Minton & Co., c.1840, 6 x 6

JS2013.527.281

Encaustic tile, The Campbell Brick & Tile Co., 1875–1882, 6 x 6

JS2013.527.282

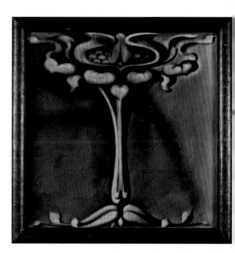

Relief-moulded Art Nouveau tile, T. & R. Boote, c.1910, 6¾ x 6¾

JS2013.527.283

I was really into Art Nouveau and continue to enjoy this restrained English design. Not so wildly swirling as the continental extravaganzas.

Hand-painted tile, Dunsmore on a G. Woolliscroft & Sons 1926 blank, 6½ x 6½

JS2013.527.319

have been captivated by this tile for over thirty years.

Glazed encaustic tile, W. Godwin, 5¼ x 5¼

JS2013.527.320

Hand-painted tile, William De Morgan, 1888–1897, 7 x 7

JS2013.527.321

The strangest ship you've ever seen – a large fish, a bow with small Gothic arches.

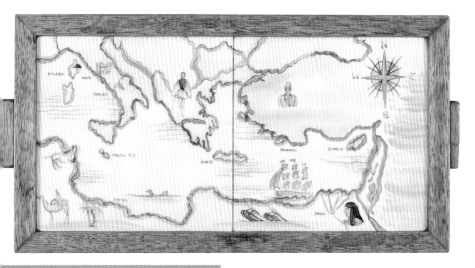

Hand-painted Mediterranean map tea tray, Packard & Ord, 13 x 7

JS2013.527.317

Relief-moulded tile, 4¼ x 4¼

JS2013.527.322

In many respects I love this tile most of all – the range of medieval colours, the variety and tone of moulding. The annual TACS Tile Fair is the happiest day of the year; better than a Rugby Varsity match. William Burges?

Hand-painted tile panel from the 'Fishermen' series, designed by Sylvia Packard for Packard & Ord on a H. & G. Thynne blank, c.1948, 13 x 6¾

JS2013.527.318

Silk-screen printed tile from the 'Coloured Dutch' series, designed by Joseph Roelants, Carter & Co., 1930s, 11 x 11

JS2013.527.324

Transfer-printed outline and hand-coloured landscape from the 'New Domesday Book of Kent' series, designed by Donald Maxwell, Doulton, 6½ x 5½

JS2013.527.323

Encaustic tile, W. Godwin, 6 x 6

JS2013.527.328

Right: Relief-moulded tile, Copeland, c.1870, 6 x 6

JS2013.527.327

A jewel-like tile. I immediately see it beside the glorious wonders of Russian and English jewellery in a recent Victoria and Albert Museum exhibition. I think it has a 'nick' but this is nothing to me. I advise collectors to buy master pieces with 'nicks'.

Silk-screen printed tile from the 'Farm' series, designed by E.E. Stickland for Carter & Co., originally designed in the 1930s, this is a later version from 1951, 9½ x 9½

JS2013.527.325

Lovely style and landscape. 'Over the hills and far away …'

Encaustic tile, Minton & Co., c.1860, 6 x 6

JS2013.527.326

Hand-painted tile, William De Morgan, 6½ x 6½

JS2013.527.329

Hand-painted tile, William De Morgan, 1888–1897, 6½ x 6½

JS2013.527.330

I think I've seen 200 varieties of ships!

Hand-painted tile, William De Morgan, 6¾ x 6¾

JS2013.527.331

These are very rare; I sense this is a stylised Aeolus, the North Wind, that endangered the lives of Aeneas and his men on their voyage.

Hand-painted tile, William De Morgan, 7 x 7

JS2013.527.332

Hand-painted tile, William De Morgan, 7 x 7

JS2013.527.333

A magnificent figurehead and two-storey castle on the poop deck.

Stencilled with hand-painted border, possibly designed by Polly Brace for Dunsmore Tiles, 7½ x 7½

JS2013.527.334

I searched for this tile for over fifty years. Then I found it damaged but much better than nothing.

Hand-painted tile, William De Morgan, 1882–1888, 6 x 6

JS2013.527.335

A lone Helmsman, a flat sea, but the sail full of wind. There are no limits to the artist's licence! The crazier the merrier for me!

Hand-painted tile, William De Morgan, 1888–1897, 7 x 7

JS2013.527.336

Another strange vessel, the stranger the better, with multi-patterned sails, and a sloppy looking hull, its portholes overly close to the waterline.

Hand-painted tile, William De Morgan, 7 x 7

JS2013.527.337

I think that I have never bought two identical ship designs.

Hand-painted tile depicting Uroborus, a snake or dragon eating its own tail to symbolise eternity, designed by William De Morgan and based on a mark he used for a period in memory of his father, 1887–1897, 8¾ x 8¾

JS2013.527.338

Funny, I will never forget this. John Cox my tile 'initiator' had a friend with this tile in a disused corner. She gave it to me. Lovely image that is typically De Morgan.

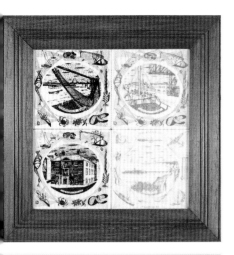

Transfer-printed tile panel, designed by Bernard Charles, Carter & Co., 1960s, 17 x 17

JS2013.527.1773

Hand-painted stencilled tile panel, designed by Polly Brace for Dunsmore Tiles, c.1930, 14½ x 14½

JS2013.527.1737

Transfer-printed and hand-painted tile, Minton Hollins & Co., 1875–1910, 12½ x 12½

JS2013.527.1736

This is a duplicate of one that is in the tile scheme of the Victoria and Albert Museum refreshment room.

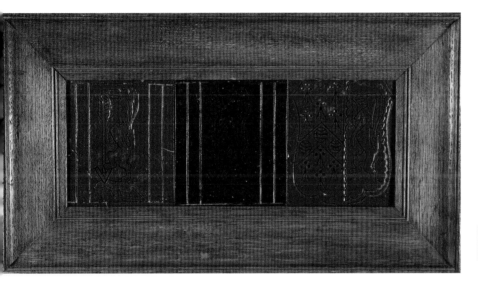

Left: Impressed line tiles, Maw & Co., 11¼ x 20½

JS2013.527.1738

Left: Designed by Lewis F. Day, Maw & Co., 15½ x 9½

JS2013.527.1735

'Every dog shall have his day.' This was Lewis F. Day's big moment! Otherwise I have always felt him second to De Morgan.

Block-printed and hand-coloured tile panel,
Minton China Works, 27½ x 12

JS2013.527.1629

Gorgeous border. Probably Dresser.
Top Twelve.

Block-printed and hand-painted tile panel,
designed by A.W.N. Pugin, Minton & Co.,
15 x 15

JS2013.527.1615

Encaustic tile panel, Minton & Co.,
15½ x 15½

JS2013.527.1626

Encaustic tile panel, Minton & Co., 1878,
16 x 16

JS2013.527.1625

Outstanding. Dresser? Top Five.

Encaustic tile panel, Minton & Co., 16 x 16

JS2013.527.1698

Hand-painted tile panel, designed by Christopher Dresser, Minton China Works, 18¾ x 19

JS2013.527.1556

Left: Encaustic tile panel, Minton & Co., 16¼ x 16¼

JS2013.527.1568

Among my Top Ten favourite encaustic panels.

Encaustic tile panel, Minton Hollins & Co., 18½ x 18½

JS2013.527.1589

I have always liked the ensembles of floor tiles in large spaces. The Birch Church in Manchester was superb. This design was a repeat from a small church and I was delighted to get a full 'picture'. Coming from Merseyside, I am much embarrassed to admit I have never seen the huge pavement in St George's Hall, Liverpool.

Designed by Alfred Waterhouse, Minton Hollins & Co., 1877, 19 x 12¾

JS2013.527.1562

Six hexagonal tiles from Old Eaton Hall demolished by the Duke of Westminster. They probably were taken from the lavatories.

Hand-painted stencilled tile panel depicting
Alice in Wonderland characters, designed
by C.F.A. Voysey after John Tenniel,
Dunsmore Tiles on Minton blanks, 1950s,
12½ x 12½

JS2013.527.1559

Encaustic tile panel, Minton & Co.,
21½ x 15

JS2013.527.1548

Encaustic tile panel, Minton & Co.,
20½ x 20½

JS2013.527.1547

In my Top Twenty and gorgeously rich. It is
amazing that this factory had such a range
of fabulous designers and craftsmen who
produced such little jewels that still delight
us today.

Block-printed pseudo-encaustic tiles,
Minton Hollins & Co., 12½ x 12½

JS2013.527.1724

Printed and hand-painted tile from the
'Early English' series, designed by Helen
J.A. Miles, Wedgwood, 21⅝ x 29¾

JS2013.527.1491

Left: Glazed encaustic tile panel, Minton &
Co., 16¾ x 16¾

JS2013.527.1560

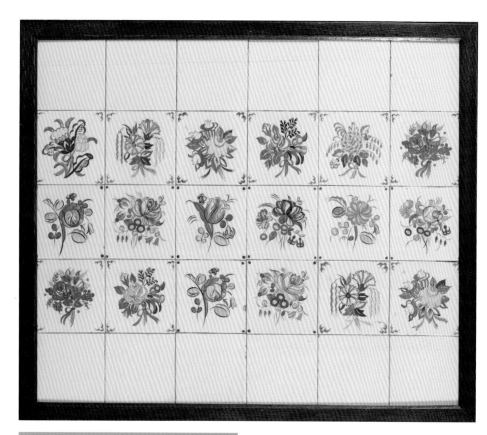

Hand-painted tiles, designed by Truda Carter, Carter & Co., 1950s, 27½ x 32½

JS2013.527.1492

Encaustic tile panel, Minton & Co., 1871, 20½ x 21

JS2013.527.1538

A consistently complicated pattern. I greatly enjoy its strangely hypnotic air.

Hand-painted tiles by Majel Davidson, J.C. Edwards (Ruabon), 1920–1930, 15½ x 15½

JS2013.527.1699

Encaustic tile panel, possibly designed by John Pollard Seddon, The Campbell Brick & Tile Co., 31 x 19½

JS2013.527.1537

A gift from Kenneth Beaulah. He could not fit this in his collection! Kenneth was the Eminence Grice of TACS and responsible for a vast number of medieval tiles given and catalogued for the British Museum. He is sorely missed.

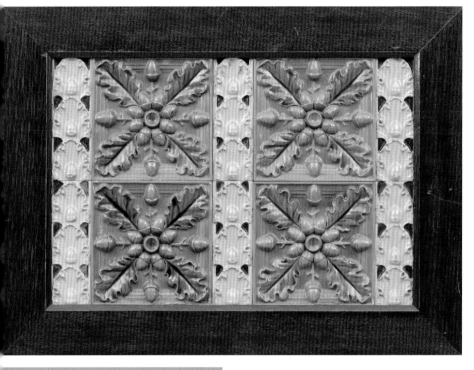

Screen-printed tile panel from the 'Mask' series, designed by Leslie Elsden, Carter & Co., 1963, 11 x 11

JS2013.527.1639

Relief-moulded tile panel, Maw & Co., 17 x 23

JS2013.527.1505

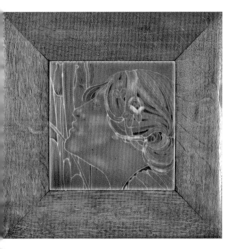

Relief-moulded Art Nouveau portrait tile, J. & W. Wade, c.1901, 11½ x 11½

JS2013.527.1650

Pierced majolica tile made for the Great Stove at the Great Exhibition, designed by A.W.N. Pugin, Minton & Co., 1851, 12 x 12

JS2013.527.1645

Pugin's Medieval Court and its Great Stove caused a sensation!

Encaustic tile panel, W. Godwin, 13¾ x 10

JS2013.527.1678

Probably Pugin.

Hand-painted tile, William De Morgan,
1888–1897, 11 x 11

JS2013.527.1651

Very rare. Deft touch.

Hand-painted tile panel designed for
W.H. Smith, Carter & Co., c.1930, 18 x 20

JS2013.527.1498

Hand-painted tile panel designed for
W.H. Smith, Carter & Co., c.1930, 21 x 21

JS2013.527.1493

Hand-painted tile, William De Morgan, 6 x 6

JS2013.527.588

Lustre tile, William De Morgan, 6½ x 6½

JS2013.527.561

Hand-painted tile, William De Morgan,
1898, 6½ x 6½

JS2013.527.562

Hand-painted tile, William De Morgan,
1888–1897, 6½ x 6½

JS2013.527.563

Hand-painted tile, William De Morgan,
1888–1897, 6½ x 6½

JS2013.527.559

Encaustic tile, 6¾ x 6¾

JS2013.527.560

Right: Encaustic tile panel, Minton & Co.,
21½ x 15½

JS2013.527.1502

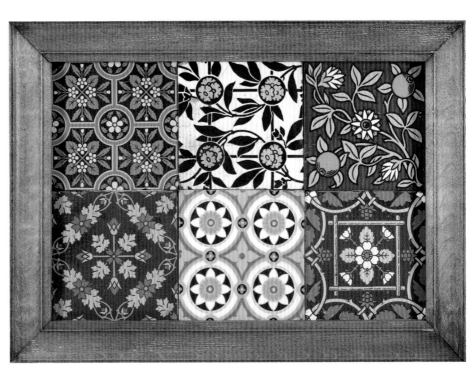

Screen-printed and hand-coloured tiles from the 'Landscape' series, designed by Dorincourt Industries on a Carter & Co. blank, 1958, 6 x 6

JS2013.527.554, JS2013.527.555, JS2013.527.556, JS2013.527.557, JS2013.527.558

I started collecting this series dreaming of finding them all. That would be a collection! However, I have not got far ... like so many things in life.

Block-printed tile, Minton Hollins & Co., 6 x 6

JS2013.527.552

Hand-painted tile, Maw & Co., 6 x 6

JS2013.527.546

Hand-painted tile, William De Morgan, 1888–1897, 6 x 6

JS2013.527.550

Hand-painted tile, William De Morgan, 7 x 7

JS2013.527.551

Hand-painted tile, William De Morgan, 1872–1881, 6 x 6

JS2013.527.548

Hand-painted tile, William De Morgan, 6¾ x 6¾

JS2013.527.549

Hand-painted tile, William De Morgan, 1888–1897, 6¾ x 6¾

JS2013.527.553

Encaustic tile, W. Godwin, 6 x 6

JS2013.527.547

Encaustic tile, Minton & Co., 6 x 6

JS2013.527.544

Transfer-printed and hand-painted tiles, Minton Hollins & Co., 8¾ x 33

JS2013.527.1779

Printed tile, Minton China Works, 6 x 6

JS2013.527.545

Encaustic tile panel, Maw & Co.,
15½ x 15½

JS2013.527.1707

Encaustic tile panel, probably Craven
Dunnill & Co., 15 x 15

JS2013.527.1700

Anthemion forever!

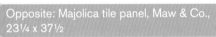

Encaustic tile panel, W. Godwin,
15½ x 15½

JS2013.527.1770

Opposite: Majolica tile panel, Maw & Co.,
23¼ x 37½

JS2013.527.1783

This is the second superb panel of Maw
& Co. majolica. I am wondering whether I
should give Ironbridge another panel. My
walls at home will be rather bare. A superb
panel that is in my Top Twenty!

Encaustic tile panel, Minton & Co.,
15¾ x 15¾

JS2013.527.1527

Right: Encaustic tile panel, W. Godwin,
10 x 10

JS2013.527.1677

Below: Hand-painted tile from the 'Toy Box'
series, designed by Dora Batty, Carter &
Co., c.1930, 4½ x 6

JS2013.527.239

Lively.

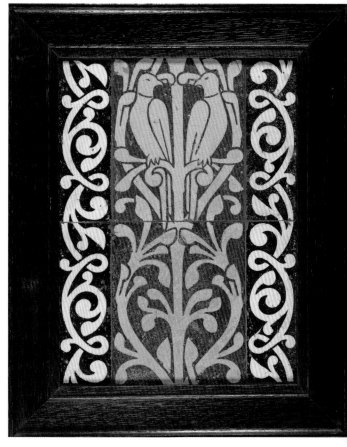

Relief-moulded tile panel, Minton China Works, 12½ x 18½

JS2013.527.1674

Opposite: Encaustic tile panel, Minton & Co., 16 x 13

JS2013.527.1727

Close to my heart. Dug them out of an abandoned church in Ealing. The border tiles are delightfully fresh and lively.

Right: Relief-moulded tile, Copeland, 1870–1900, 6 x 6

JS2013.527.246

An exquisite tile in fine relief.

THE JOHN SCOTT TILE COLLECTION

Opposite: Hand-painted tile panel, William De Morgan, 1888–1897, 21½ x 15½

JS2013.527.1579

had five of these for twenty years or so and was then given the missing one by Jon Catleugh. Top Seven.

Encaustic tile, W. Godwin, 5¾ diameter

JS2013.527.237

Hand-painted tile, designed by Majel Davidson, c.1930, 6 x 6

JS2013.527.238

Unusual and stylish.

Hand-painted tile, William De Morgan, 1898, 6½ x 6½

JS2013.527.240

Rather unusual and zany.

Hand-painted tile, William De Morgan, 1888–1897, 6¾ x 6¾

JS2013.527.235

Hand-painted tile, William De Morgan design using an Architectural Pottery Co. blank, 6½ x 6½

JS2013.527.236

Right: Encaustic tile, designed by John Pollard Seddon, W. Godwin, 15 x 15

JS2013.527.1683

I have been waiting thirty years for the rest of this panel.

Hand-painted tile, William De Morgan, 6½ x 6½

JS2013.527.241

Hand-painted tile, William De Morgan, 1898, 6¾ x 6¾

JS2013.527.242

Hand-painted tile, William De Morgan, 1882–1888, 6¾ x 6¾

JS2013.527.243

Hand-painted tile, William De Morgan, 1898, 6 x 6

JS2013.527.247

Hand-painted tile, William De Morgan, 1888–1897, 6¾ x 6¾

JS2013.527.249

Hand-painted tile, William De Morgan, 1882–1888, 6¾ x 6¾

JS2013.527.250

Hand-painted tile, designed and painted by F.G. Cooper, 7 x 7

JS2013.527.248

Contemporary. I just liked it.

Glazed encaustic tile, Minton Hollins & Co., 1860, 4 x 4

JS2013.527.245

Glazed encaustic tile, W. Godwin, 4 x 4

JS2013.527.244

Transfer-printed tile panel, designed by
William Wise, Minton China Works, 16 x 16

JS2013.527.1697

Excellent example of William Wise's mastery
of country scenes.

Hand-painted tin-glazed tile panel from the
'Dogs' series, designed by Cecil Aldin,
Carter & Co., c.1935, 18½ x 7½

JS2013.527.1523

Not my usual preference but Cecil Aldin is a
master draftsman of dogs.

Encaustic tile panel, Robert Minton Taylor &
Co., 14½ x 14½

JS2013.527.1682

Left: Hand-painted tile panel, made for
W.H. Smith, Carter & Co., c.1930,
11¾ x 25

JS2013.527.1554

Tile panel, designed by Lewis F. Day, Pilkington, 21 x 15

JS2013.527.1543

I must admit that I am generally not too keen on Lewis F. Day. I quite like them but they lack the zip and quirkiness of De Morgan or Dresser. I still collect them!

Right: Hand-painted tile panel, designed by Truda Carter, 1950s, 15 x 21

JS2013.527.1542

Extra blanks came in 'the lot' so I juxtaposed them in this way. A lot of display is personal choice. That is the essence of collecting tiles.

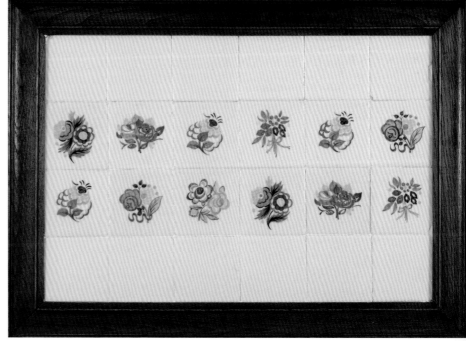

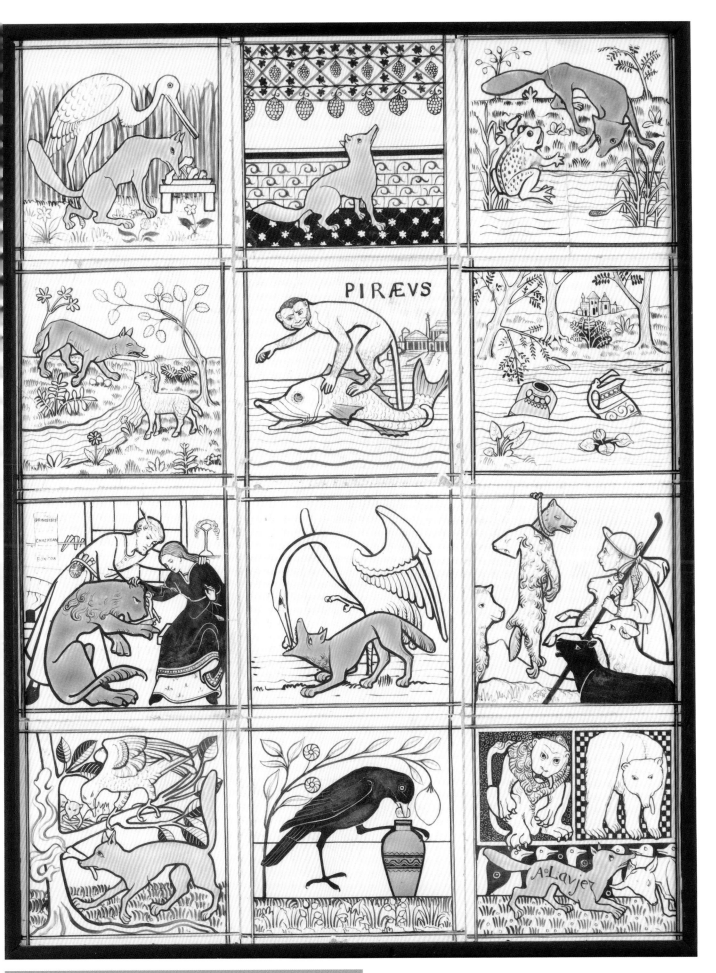

Aesop's Fables, designed by A. Lavjer, Minton Hollins & Co., 19 x 24¾

Relief-moulded tile panel, Minton & Co.,
25½ x 25½

JS2013.527.1574

Outstandingly luxurious and exquisitely
beautiful – in my Top Ten. This image
reminds me of the climax of Edgar Allan
Poe's *The Domain of Arnheim*. The magical
domain is a mixture of many styles each
adding to the magnificence of the whole.
And this is how I feel. This is an industrial,
albeit hand-painted product using the most
beautiful of 19th-century English tiles. A truly
lyrical spectacle.

LEGACY

My collection is merely a few snapshots of a long film … there is huge area of choice for new tile collectors … good hunting to you.

John Scott, 2013

John Scott would like to inspire others to collect. He sees collecting as a pastime that is stimulating and rewarding for the individual. He also believes that collections should eventually be given to museums for others to enjoy.

Each tile within John Scott's collection has special meaning and significance to him. Some remind him of old friends, whilst others recall particular times in his life. Thanks to his generous donation and philanthropic beliefs, his collection can now be seen and enjoyed by many thousands of people every year at Jackfield Tile Museum.

Even now John has not stopped collecting and continues to add to the material that he has given to the Trust. John is also keen that this collection be improved upon with further donations, research and study.

John Scott's legacy, an infectious enthusiasm for collecting, support for the Museum and for making collections publicly accessible will have a lasting impact on the world of decorative arts.

A set of stencilled tiles designed by the Surrealist artist Salvador Dali. Made at the El Siglio tile factory, Onda, Spain, 1954. These are the most recent additions to the collection, bought by John Scott in 2014.

JS2014.350.1, JS2014.350.2, JS2014.350.3, JS2013.350.4, JS2014.350.5, JS2014.350.6

POST-MORTEM OBITUARY

Encaustic tile, Minton & Co., 6 x 6

JS2013.527.532

This is my favourite encaustic; its black field invites a great design. So simple, so timeless. No. 1.

I am left with some poignant thoughts at the end. Firstly, thank you to Anna Brennand and Gillian Crumpton, and the team at the Ironbridge Gorge Museum Trust, for a superb collaboration and hard work. I'm a pernickety old man … and I am delighted. A few tiles are duplicated but it is a gorgeous display.

My strongest unfulfilled desire is to be guardian of Valhalla! – the sacred home of the art produced by my heroes: Pugin, Guimard, Gilbert, Knox, De Morgan, Street, Harry Clarke, the Martin Brothers and many others, but above all Christopher Dresser. I want to place him on the pedestal he deserves, amongst the pantheon of the great names that enriched the greatest empire in the world in Victorian times. The ultimate mystery is how William Morris scraped his way ahead of this pure genius! I hope many of you will share my love of tile designs. Aren't they marvellous? I believe Dresser designed many of the best. I am asked for my favourites and add 'top 5' or 'top 10'. As I gaze in wonder and delight in a state of drugged intoxication, it is hard to relegate any below the highest categories.

My ambition is to laud and extol the achievement of those who built our heritage. Walk down Fulham Palace Road and delight at the 1880 terraced homes, front gardens, cast-iron railings, stone piers, stained-glass porches, terracotta gable ends, brass or iron door furniture and … tiles galore: polychrome Minton encaustics in the porch to hand-painted panels beside the front door.

I have another interest in the modern world: involvement in the public domain. Currently I am trying to persuade the Natural History Museum to restore and repaint its magnificent boundary railing (Cromwell Road) a red/rust tone … not black. A scrape of the paint shows a red/rust colour for the original year c.1880. I think this would look significantly better than the black proposed. It's a very difficult battle which I shall probably lose, but …

Collecting is a broad church. Very personal; and it is perhaps selfish as the aim is to please yourself. You may not aspire to or acquire the glory of Duveen, Jacques Doucet, Bob Walker or Charles Handley-Read, but you will make lots of friends and interests. The current boom in contemporary art is a sign of the enormous boom in the boundaries of collecting.

You will never be bored.

John Scott, November 2016

MEDUSA AND THE LOST FLOOR OF CLIVEDEN

Encaustic tile depicting Medusa, Minton & Co., 1895, 15 diameter

JS2013.527.1595

This was the centrepiece of a large floor ordered by the American millionaire, Mr Astor, for his residence at Cliveden, Buckinghamshire. My most lucky find. Not quite Tutankhamun's death mask but still … Bought from dealer in Jones Arcade and previously owned by the daughter of the surveyor supervising the improvements at Cliveden in 1904. The head of Medusa is the centrepiece … The destruction of this floor tops the list of awful losses of much of Britain's cultural heritage. I weep.

The encaustic pavement of Cliveden was described in *The Pottery Gazette*, 1 November 1895:

Millionaire's Encaustic Floor

Some years ago, the late Mr. Herbert Minton presented to the then Duchess of Sutherland an elaborately manufactured encaustic tile floor for her residence at Clevedon, Bucks, and the property having passed into the possession of Mr. Astor, the American millionaire, that gentleman has recently ordered a counterpart of it from the present firm of Messrs. Minton, Hollins, & Co., of Stoke-upon-Trent, and which we have had the privilege of seeing. The floor is 25 ft. 8 in. by 23 ft. 8 in., and is of a most artistic character and wonderfully displays the high manufacturing powers of the firm. The whole floor has been specially designed and modelled, and is undoubtedly the finest of its kind ever produced. The Corinthian form of design is mainly adopted. On the outer border of the floor are Cupids allegorically drawn. The base of the ornament on the outer edge is of a jasper blue colour, the figures of the Cupids being white, and in their hands they hold a wreath, the ends of which are attached to a vase in the form of a fountain. A scroll and a key border are also effectively introduced. At the top of the columns or plinths in the centre of the floor are allegorical figures in white upon a jasper ground, the figures being relieved by touches of green. The elements are represented by four allegorical pictures, and in the centre of the pavement the mask of Medusa is portrayed. The colours of the tiles used in the construction of this beautiful work of art are blue, white, grey, buffs, black, green, and purple. It is impossible to convey by description anything like an adequate idea of the rare beauty which the design presents to the eye, or of the harmonious colouring which has been attained by the firm in this their distinctive branch of the ceramic art. The entrance hall to Clevedon when this pavement is laid will consist of 60 ft. by 25 ft. of Messrs. Minton, Hollins, & Co.'s tiles, and will have a most magnificent appearance, such, in fact, as no other palatial residence in the kingdom can present.

American millionaire William Waldorf Astor bought Cliveden in 1893 for $1.2m and set about remodelling many rooms of the house and improving the grounds. Astor's eldest son, Waldorf, married Nancy Langhorne in 1906 and they were given Cliveden as a wedding gift. Nancy Astor reputedly did not like the Minton encaustic floor and had it taken up and stored in the basement of the property. Waldorf Astor gave Cliveden to the National Trust in 1942 and in 1966 it was opened to the public.

The Ironbridge Gorge Museum Trust and the National Trust are working in partnership to reunite the Medusa centrepiece tile from the John Scott Collection with its border tiles. It is hoped that this will then be displayed at both venues to showcase not only the beautiful encaustic tiles but also the collaborative work between the Ironbridge Gorge Museums and the National Trust.

MANUFACTURERS
AND DESIGNERS

The following section lists some of the key manufacturers and designers involved in the tile industry from 1830 to the 1980s. The selected bibliography provides sources for further information.

Edward Bawden

Edward Bawden (1903–1989) was an English printmaker, graphic designer, illustrator, war artist and painter. He designed for the tile company Carter & Co. His work is distinctive: simple lines that convey energy, irony and humour. His tile designs also often provide a comment on the English class system, which perhaps reflects his struggle with class in his early life.

Carter & Co.

Carter & Co. of Poole, Dorset, was established by Jesse Carter in 1873. It became one of the finest tile and architectural ceramics companies in England. It was known for its lustre ware and decorative pottery. Carter & Co. also made blank tiles for William De Morgan from the early 1870s.

During the 1920s and up to the 1950s its unique and often whimsical tile designs can be attributed to a group of diverse and talented artists, including Dora Batty, Edward Bawden, Harold Stabler, Truda Carter, Reginald Till, E.E. Stickland, Cecil Aldin, and Alfred Read.

Poole Pottery, as Carter & Co. became known, is still a household name, and since its early days has created a strong and distinctive form of British pottery and ceramics.

Kenneth and Ann Clark

Kenneth Clark MBE (1922–2012) was a pioneering ceramicist, tile maker and influential author on the subject. Kenneth Clark Ceramics operated between 1952 and 2004. Ann Clark (*née* Wynn-Reeves), his wife, was the principal designer for the company. Their strong partnership and fresh contemporary and innovative designs account for their success in both domestic and large-scale contexts.

Craven Dunnill & Co.

Craven Dunnill & Co. was established in 1871. It emerged from various partnerships established in the early 1860s (Hawes, Denny & Hargreaves; Hargreaves & Craven; and Hargreaves, Craven Dunnill & Co.). In 1872 Charles Lynam was commissioned to design a new purpose-built factory at Jackfield, Shropshire. Craven Dunnill & Co. produced wall and floor tiles until 1950 when it became a distributor for other tile manufacturers, and moved to Bridgnorth. In 2000 Craven Dunnill Jackfield Ltd moved back to its original factory, now within Jackfield Tile Museum, and began manufacturing period-style tiles. Chris Cox leads the encaustic tile department and they are currently working on major restoration projects, including the Palace of Westminster.

Christopher Dresser

Christopher Dresser (1834–1904) studied at the Government School of Design in London, which had been established to train designers for industry. His studio had a huge output, creating designs for metalwork, textiles, wallpaper and ceramics, including tiles. He worked for a large number of manufacturers in Britain, France, Japan and the USA.

Dresser was inspired by classical, Gothic, Islamic and Ancient Egyptian styles. He embraced mass production but also wanted to raise the standard of products for the consumer markets. Dresser was interested in the art and culture of Japan, which culminated in his visit there in 1876. He was the first European designer to be commissioned by the British government to visit Japan. The profound effect of the aesthetic of Japan is clear in much of his work. He is regarded as the first professional industrial designer.

Godwin

Originally making bricks, quarry tiles and drainpipes, the company of William Godwin began manufacturing encaustic tiles in the 1850s. In 1881 William's son, William Henry Godwin, entered into partnership, creating the company W. Godwin & Son. They produced an extensive range of tiles for floors and walls. By 1906 the business had been sold to G.H. Lloyd and Thomas Pulling. In 1912 it was purchased by Mr T.E. Davies who continued to trade as William Godwin & Son, Lugwardine Tile Works Ltd. J.G.M. Jeffrey and his son J.R.M. Jeffrey joined the business in 1922 but by 1927 the works was sold to H. & G. Thynne Ltd.

The Victoria Tile Works was set up by Henry Godwin in direct competition with his brother William in 1876. In 1884 William Hewitt joined the company forming Godwin & Hewitt. Henry Godwin sold his share of the business to William Hewitt in 1894. In 1907 this company was also bought by H. & G. Thynne Ltd.

Maw & Co.

In 1850 John Hornby Maw bought the stock of the Worcester tile works Fleming St John and G. Barr, Chamberlain & Co. and handed production to his two sons, George and Arthur. In 1852 they moved their works to Broseley in Shropshire and established the Maw & Co. Benthall Encaustic Tile Works. They engaged Charles Lynam to design a new factory and by 1883 Maw & Co. had moved into its new works. By 1900 it was the largest tile company in the world. It continued to make tiles until 1968 when it was absorbed into H. & R. Johnson and the factory at Jackfield closed.

Minton

Thomas Minton established Minton in 1793; his son Herbert Minton began the company's involvement in tile manufacture and the company was at the forefront of tile production. Michael Daintry Hollins joined the firm in 1845. Originally the tile company had two divisions: Minton & Co. was responsible for floor tiles, whilst wall tiles were sold under the name Minton, Hollins and Co. However, in 1868 the company formally split. A series of lawsuits and disputes over company names ensued. Three distinct companies emerged: Minton Hollins & Co., which also traded as Minton & Co. until its demise in 1968; Robert Minton Taylor & Co.; and Minton China Works. Colin Minton Campbell, operating Minton China Works, bought out Robert Minton Taylor and formed Minton Brick & Tile Co. By 1875 Campbell was trading as The Campbell Brick & Tile Co. and Minton China Works. In 1918 Minton China Works stopped its production of tiles but The Campbell Brick & Tile Co. continued until its merger with H. & R. Johnson in 1962.

William De Morgan

William De Morgan (1839–1917) was an Arts and Crafts artist and designer. He was introduced to William Morris in 1863 and shared his ideals of craft traditions. De Morgan began designing tiles in the 1860s and experimented with glazes and colours. Whilst some of his motifs were influenced by Morris, most of De Morgan's pieces were more flamboyant, dramatic and fantastic. They had their influence in medieval manuscripts and the ancient arts of Persia and the Far East. His tile designs, which number over 1,000, feature vivid patterns of leaves, flowers, birds, monsters, ships and animals. In 1907 William De Morgan stopped making pottery and left his Fulham works. He continued his life as a successful novelist.

William Morris

William Morris (1834–1896) was the central figure of the Arts and Crafts movement which developed in Britain during the late 19th century. It was a reaction against the Industrial Revolution and mass production, and instead idealised medieval craftsmanship. Morris wrote and lectured on Arts and Crafts philosophy and style. His company, founded in 1861, created designs for textiles, furniture, glass and tiles. His delicate patterns and colours, inspired by nature, were in contrast to those produced using printing technology.

A.W.N. Pugin

Augustus Welby Northmore Pugin (1812–1852) was an influential architect, designing over 100 buildings. He also wrote several important books on Gothic architecture and style. He worked with the architect Charles Barry in designing the interior of the Palace of Westminster from 1844. He also organised the Medieval Court display at the Great Exhibition of 1851. His early death at the age of 40 is often attributed to exhaustion, such was his work ethic and design output.

Pugin was inspired by the medieval Gothic style of architecture and design, and became the leading figure in the Gothic Revival. His association with the Minton & Co. tile works was particularly important as Pugin believed that encaustic tiles were essential to the Gothic interior. This style was influenced by the medieval use of bold colours, strong designs, and religious and heraldic imagery.

John Pollard Seddon

John Pollard Seddon (1827–1906) was an architect and designer. He favoured the Gothic style of architecture and this influenced his work as he advocated simple lines and traditional construction. He was elected a Fellow of the Royal Institute of British Architects in 1860, and had a flourishing architectural practice in the 1860s and early 1870s. He also restored medieval churches and published several books.

C.F.A. Voysey

Charles Francis Annesley Voysey (1857–1941) was an Arts and Crafts architect and designer. Voysey was a pupil of John Pollard Seddon, an architect of the Gothic Revival, from 1874 to 1879. He started his own architectural and design practice in 1881, and was a regular exhibitor at the Royal Academy. He was a member of the Art Workers' Guild and became a Fellow of the Royal Institute of British Architects in 1929. He was awarded the Royal Gold Medal for architecture in 1940.

Voysey was influenced by William Morris and the Arts and Crafts movement, but also by the simplicity and natural forms used within the Art Nouveau style. He was convinced that simplicity in decoration was essential for creating rich designs. He drew inspiration from nature and promoted the use of traditional materials in craft and architecture.

GLOSSARY

Encaustic

The word encaustic comes from the Greek word meaning 'to burn in'. Different colours of clay are used to create an encaustic tile and the design is within the body of the tile rather than being applied as surface decoration.

Clay is pressed into a mould – different coloured clays can be used at this stage to make a multi-coloured design. A layer of clay is then applied to create the thickness of the tile. The tile is removed from the mould leaving an embedded pattern in the clay. Liquid clay called 'slip' is then poured over the whole surface of the tile, filling in the recesses in the pattern. Once the tile is dry, the excess clay is scraped off the surface to reveal the pattern underneath. The tile is then fired.

Tube-lined

Liquid or slip clay is piped onto a tile to form raised lines that create a pattern and areas where coloured glazes can be applied. The slip acts as a barrier and stops the glazes melting into one another.

Relief-moulded

Clay is either pressed or poured into a mould to form a tile with a raised design. Once fired, the tile can be decorated with glazes and is then ready for its final firing.

Transfer-printed

This is the process whereby an image from a metal plate, wood block or lithographic stone is applied to the surface of a tile using a medium such as tissue or gelatine before firing.

Screen-printed

An image is directly printed onto a tile often using a frame covered in silk that has either a stencil or gelatine pattern. Colour is pushed through the screen and transfers the design to the tile.

SELECTED BIBLIOGRAPHY

Atterbury, Paul & Irvine, Louise. *The Doulton Story*. Stoke on Trent: Royal Doulton Tableware Limited, 1979

Baeck, Mario, Hamburg, Ulrich, Rabenau, Thomas & Verbrugge, Bart. *Industrial Tiles 1840–1940*. Edited by Johan Kamermans & Hans van Lemmen. Otterlo: Nederlands Tegelmuseum, 2004

Barnard, Julian. *Victorian Ceramic Tiles*. London: Cassell, 1979 reprint

Blanchett, Chris. *20th Century Decorative British Tiles, Commercial Manufacturers A–H*. Pennsylvania: Schiffer Publishing Ltd, 2006

——. *20th Century Decorative British Tiles, Commercial Manufacturers J–W*. Pennsylvania: Schiffer Publishing Ltd, 2006

——. *20th Century Decorative British Tiles, Craft & Studio Tile Makers*. Pennsylvania: Schiffer Publishing Ltd, 2006

Blanchett, Chris & van Lemmen, Hans. *20th Century Tiles*. Oxford: Shire Publications, 1999

Calloway, Stephen & Federle Orr, Lynn, assisted by Esmé Whittaker. *The Cult of Beauty, The Aesthetic Movement 1860–1900*. London: V&A Publications, 2002

Catleugh, Jon. *William De Morgan Tiles*. Somerset: Richard Dennis, 1991

Graves, Alun. *Tiles and Tilework*. London: V&A Publications, 2002

Greene, John. *Brightening the Long Days, Hospital Picture Tiles*. Gloucester: Tiles and Architectural Society with Alan Sutton Publishing, 1987

Greensted, Mary. *The Arts and Crafts Movement in Britain*. Oxford: Shire Publications, 2014

Greenwood, Martin. *The Designs of William De Morgan*. Somerset: Richard Dennis, 2007

Halen, Widar. *Christopher Dresser: A Pioneer of Modern Design*. Phaidon Press, 1994

Hayward, Leslie. *Poole Pottery, Carter & Company and their Successors 1873–2011*. Edited by Paul Atterbury. Somerset: Richard Dennis, 2011

Herbert, Tony & Huggins, Kathryn. *The Decorative Tile in Architecture and Interiors*. London: Phaidon Press Limited, 1995, reprinted 2000

Morley, Christopher. *Dresser's Decorative Design*. Beresford C, 2010

Myers, Richard & Hilary. *William Morris Tiles*. Somerset: Richard Dennis, 1996

Pearson, Lynn (ed.). *Tile Gazetteer, A Guide to British Tile and Architectural Ceramics Locations*. Somerset: The Tiles & Architectural Ceramics Society and Lynn Pearson with Richard Dennis, 2005

Van Lemmen, Hans. *Victorian Tiles*. Oxford: Shire Publications, 1981

——. *Decorative Tiles Throughout the Ages*. London: Bracken Books, 1988

——. *Art Nouveau Tiles*. Oxford: Shire Publications, 2012

——. *Art Deco Tiles*. Oxford: Shire Publications, 2012

——. *5000 Years of Tiles*. London: The British Museum Press, 2013

Van Lemmen, Hans & Malam, John (eds). *Fired Earth, 1000 Years of Tiles in Europe*. Somerset: Richard Dennis, 1991

Whiteway, Michael (ed.). *Christopher Dresser, A Design Revolution*. London: V&A Publications in association with Cooper-Hewitt, National Design Museum, 2004

Yorke, Malcolm. *Edward Bawden & His Circle*. Suffolk: Antique Collectors' Club, 2007, reprinted 2010